DOLLARS
AND ENE

DOLLARS AND ENE

*Protecting Your Money
and Making It Grow*

A UNIQUE PRIMER
FOR THE INDIVIDUAL INVESTOR

by

BETTY WULIGER

Random House   New York

Every effort has been made to check the facts and information in this book with reliable sources, but the reader should be cautioned that such information is constantly changing and being revised.

Library of Congress Cataloging in Publication Data

Wuliger, Betty, 1921–
Dollars and ene.

1. Investments—Handbooks, manuals, etc. I. Title.
HG4521.W764   332.6'78   76–14174
ISBN 0–394–40221–9

Manufactured in the United States of America
2 4 6 8 9 7 5 3

ACKNOWLEDGMENTS

To my daughter, Betsy, for the idea for this book as well as her constant help; to my son, Frank III, for his help and encouragement; to my Mother, for developing my interest in investment finance and for her hours of listening; to my Dad, for giving me his expertise in real estate; and to the helping hands, of Laurel Strull, Bruce Stiglitz, Harold Shapero, Sam Grodin and Myron Slobodien.

Special thanks to Bob Loomis, my editor, who was my guiding light; to Gordon Molson, my agent, for believing in me; to Evelyn Walden and Sandy Christensen, my typists, who gave above and beyond the call of duty; to my family, for their moral support; and to many friends and professionals who contributed so generously of their time and information.

To my husband, Frank,
whose love and understanding has made
a difficult task so much easier

CONTENTS

DOLLARS
AND ENE

1

There's More to Investing Than Savings Accounts and Stocks

Most people prepare themselves for a vocation which provides them with a living, but few people prepare themselves for investing part of the income they earn. Instead, they invest in the easiest and most obvious ways—in savings accounts and stocks. Although this limited investment knowledge worked when corporate growth dominated the U.S. economy, it's no longer enough. Why? Because the economic situation has changed. Now the U.S. government dominates the economy. Uncle Sam is the largest employer as well as the largest borrower and he influences interest rates as well. As a result, your investment thinking must be different. You need to know more if you want to invest your money successfully.

You need to know how to choose a bank more carefully and how to be more selective in the stocks you buy, and you need to know about many other investments that are now a mystery to you. These other investments are the ones that knowledgeable investors, controlling huge amounts of money, have been buying.

3

But you as individuals can buy them also. For example, in the mid-1970s, the "big boys" were buying billions of dollars of Treasury securities—investments guaranteed by the U.S. government which were paying over 9% annually (plus tax benefits). Yet many individuals had hardly heard about them and certainly didn't know how to buy them on their own. That's what this book is all about. It is for you—the general public. It intends to give you the information you need to invest your money safely and more profitably, information which would be difficult, if not impossible, to get on your own.

Dollars and ene is not a textbook—it is an action book. It actually shows you how to use investments to your advantage, how to buy them on your own and how to compare them. All explanations are practical and in the simplest terms possible, and no previous investment experience is necessary to understand them.

This book is particularly valuable for women. Although for years women have reportedly owned over 75% of the nation's wealth, they were not in control of this money; rather, it was in their name only. Today, women are in a new position, earning more and controlling more money. As a result, it is necessary for women as well as men to know how to invest.

Investing is actually shopping. But in order to be an astute shopper, you must know your choices. *Dollars and ene* presents investment choices in the suggested order for building a sound investment program. One helpful hint: All investments are either loaning your money or owning with your money. Loaning your money is safer because all your money will be repaid in the future—but your profits are limited. Owning with your money has more risk because you do not have a guarantee of repayment in the future—but your profits are unlimited.

You can start an investment program by loaning money to either a bank (depositing savings in passbook

savings accounts) or to the U.S. government (by purchasing savings bonds). These investments are made
with money you set aside for day-to-day living expenses
and emergencies because they pay you interest and
they allow you to withdraw money easily (whenever
you want) without penalty.

Next, you can loan money to governments, government agencies or corporations (including banks) for a
specific period of time. Because these investments
guarantee the repayment of your original savings in the
future they are earmarked for later necessities (such as
your retirement plan or your children's education). In
the meantime, they pay you a guaranteed annual income—higher than the income you would receive from
passbook savings accounts or savings bonds.

Then, when you feel financially and emotionally prepared to risk money, you are ready to assume the risk
of ownership by purchasing stocks, warrants, options
and commodities. Although these investments are the
most tempting and the most talked about, they do not
guarantee the repayment of your original savings. Instead, you receive money for their value only when you
sell these investments to other investors. If you sell to
other investors for more than your original cost you
make a profit (sometimes 100%, 200% or even 300%),
whereas if you sell to other investors for less than your
original cost you take a loss (sometimes part or all of
your original investment).

During inflationary times, investments need inflation
protection. Why? Because by the time you are repaid
or sell investments, the money you receive will probably buy less. Therefore, we will also discuss ways to
protect dollars from losing purchasing power.

Lessons have been handed down from one genera-
tion to another. One such lesson, in the fable "The
Tortoise and the Hare," is most appropriate for investors. The hares are the investors in a hurry. They con-

stantly chase stock prices, then they switch to commodity exchanges and from there head to the option exchanges. The hares rush from one investment to another searching for the Never-Never Land. The tortoises, on the other hand, slowly accumulate three to six months' income in a savings account or in savings bonds. Then they buy investments that repay their original savings in the future, continually reinvesting the annual income they receive. In this way the tortoises slowly but surely double their money every seven to eight years and quadruple their money every fourteen to sixteen years. When the tortoises are financially and emotionally ready to take more risk (on the chance of making a larger profit), they buy stocks, warrants, options and even commodities. As in the fable, the conscientious tortoises generally finish way ahead of the greedy hares.

In other words, invest slowly and carefully—build a solid investment foundation. In addition, go slowly when you read about the various investments—study each investment thoroughly before you begin the next one. Learning to invest will be well worth your time and effort. It won't be very long before you, too, realize that when you work for a day you are paid for a day, whereas when you invest money wisely you are paid for a lifetime.

2

Should You Deposit Your Money in Commercial Banks? Savings and Loan Associations? Swiss Banks?

You keep money in banks because they are conveniently located, they make it easy for you to deposit or withdraw money, and because bank accounts are federally insured. You can deposit money in commercial banks, which offer both checking and savings accounts, or in savings and loan associations (S&Ls) or mutual savings banks, both of which usually offer only savings accounts.

When you deposit money in a bank, you are loaning your money to that bank in return for interest earnings. The bank, in turn, earns money by reloaning your money to corporations and individuals at a higher rate of interest than it pays you. The more deposits a bank has to reloan, the more profit it can make. That's why banks constantly try to attract new depositors by advertising, by opening convenient branches, by offering free services and by giving away bonus gifts. In other words, banking is a two-way street. On the one hand,

banks offer you a safe and convenient place to keep
your money and pay you interest on savings accounts,
and on the other, you offer banks the use of your
money, which they reloan to make a profit.

In the 1930s, after more than 9,000 U.S. banks had
failed, the federal government set up regulations determining what banks could do to prevent a similar situation from happening in the future. By the 1970s, many
of these rules had outlived their usefulness. As a result,
in 1976, government regulations were in the process of
being overhauled by Congress. But once you know the
questions to ask banks—exactly what federal insurance
offers you and what the fine print in your bankbook says
—you will be able to look out for your own banking
interests whether banking rules are changed or not.

We are going to discuss how to use banks to your
advantage. Three types of banks will be covered: commercial banks, savings banks (using S&Ls as an example) and foreign banks (using Swiss banks as an example).

COMMERCIAL BANKS

Commercial banks (also called trust companies and
community banks) offer full banking services: checking
accounts, savings accounts, investment departments
and trust departments. A commercial bank can be your
financial home, but it must be a safe one.

Why You Must Be Careful Choosing a Bank
Banks have problems, particularly when the economy
weakens. Some banks have bad loans that are uncollect-
ible as well as large losses in their investment portfolios.
Inflation robs banks of savings; when the cost of living
constantly increases, people find it impossible to save.
In addition, the U.S. government sets the maximum

interest rates that banks can pay on savings accounts under $100,000. When these rates are not competitive with other investments (as occurred in 1974) people withdraw their savings from banks to invest elsewhere. Banks with solid foundations are usually less affected by these problems, and for that reason you should choose your bank carefully.

Choosing Your Financial Home

You should choose your financial home with as much care as you choose your residential home. Just as you would not move into a residential home if it were sinking in a swamp, do not deposit money in a financial home unless it has a solid foundation.

What banks have solid foundations? *Well-managed, large national banks (with deposits of $500 million or more) and less than 70% of their deposits in loans are more likely to have solid foundations.* Here's why. Well-managed banks have a history of profitable operations; thus they are better prepared to cope with new problems. Large national banks are supervised by the National Bank Surveillance System. This agency was established in 1975 (after the failures of Franklin National Bank and U.S. National Bank of San Diego) to detect failing banks sooner and to prevent failures of major national banks. Furthermore, national banks are examined regularly by the Comptroller of the Currency. Finally, all national banks are members of the Federal Reserve System, which allows them to borrow from Federal Reserve Banks if ever necessary, and national banks are also members of the Federal Deposit Insurance Corporation (FDIC), which federally insures their deposits. Banks that are members of the FDIC pay insurance premiums annually—about 1/30 of 1% of their insured deposits. Then, should a bank fail, the FDIC promises to repay individual depositors up to a $40,000 limit on each account.

Although many depositors think a guarantee by the FDIC is a guarantee by the U.S. government, it is not. The FDIC is a self-supporting federal corporation with limited borrowing privileges from the U.S. Treasury. In 1975, the FDIC had less than 2% of its total insured deposits in its insurance fund and was authorized to borrow only $3 billion from the U.S. Treasury, which was less than 1% of its insured deposits.

From 1934, when the FDIC was established, until 1976, there was neither a severe depression nor a financial crisis. During these years few banks failed. Thus, when they did, the FDIC was able to honor all insured bank accounts immediately without having to use its borrowing authority from the Treasury. If, in a financial crisis, the FDIC needed more money to repay depositors, the U.S. government would probably feel a moral obligation to loan more money; however, the government is not required to do so. Therefore, although federally insured bank accounts are safe under normal circumstances, they do not offer the absolute safety of U.S. government securities (see Chapter 3).

You should also be aware of the fact that federally insured banks can require a thirty-day written notice (sometimes longer) before you can withdraw money from your savings account. Although banks would rarely enforce this right, it exists and can be used at their discretion. For example, suppose a bank receives a flood of requests for cash withdrawals from depositors which exceeds the bank's cash-on-hand. Even though this bank has loans outstanding to creditworthy individuals or corporations that will repay their loans when they come due in the future, the bank may not be able to get cash for these good loans immediately. Therefore, a bank could make you wait for your money while it tries to raise the additional cash it needs to meet the heavy withdrawal requests.

Commercial banks that are not overloaned are less

likely to be in that position. That is why it is important for you to check your bank and see it has no more than 70% of its deposits in loans. This leaves no less than 30% of its deposits in liquid assets. Liquid assets are securities that the bank can usually sell at a moment's notice for cash that can then be used to repay its depositors.

It is relatively easy to check the percentage of a bank's deposits in loans. You merely call any bank and request its annual statement. At first glance, the annual statement has the appearance of being written in a foreign language, but don't let this intimidate you. All you need are the first two numbers of the TOTAL DEPOSITS (found under "liabilities" because the bank owes this money to depositors) and the first four numbers of TOTAL LOANS (found under "assets" because corporations and individuals owe this money to the bank). For example, if a bank's total deposits are $4,-688,236,400—write 46; and if its total loans are $2,-875,570,000—write 28.75 (be sure you put a decimal point after the first two numbers). Now divide the loans (28.75) by the deposits (46).

$$\frac{28.75 \ (\text{loans})}{46 \ (\text{deposits})} = .62 \ (\text{or } 62\% \text{ of its deposits in loans})$$

This bank, which has 62% of its deposits in loans and 38% of its deposits in liquid assets, is more likely to repay your money whenever you want it.

How do you locate well-managed, large national banks? Call any local commercial bank for the address or telephone number of the nearest Federal Reserve Bank (or branch), which will give you a list of the large national banks in your area. Call any of these banks and request its annual report. Then check in the annual report for the percentage of its deposits in loans as well as for its record of profits for the past several years. This will reflect how well the bank has been managed.

Types of Commercial Bank Accounts

Checking accounts offered by commercial banks are a convenient way to pay your bills and to maintain orderly financial records. Your cancelled checks are legal proof of the payment of your bills. Before opening a checking account, find out what the charges (if any) are.

Since 1933, federal law has prohibited banks from paying interest on checking accounts. However, in the 1970s, some banks were getting around this law by offering combination savings and checking accounts (for example, United Security accounts offered by Citizens Bank & Trust Company of Chicago and the Combo accounts offered by Citibank of New York). Then other banks, in order to compete with the new savings-checking account, began offering free checking accounts.

Banks also offer several savings plans whose interest varies in five different ways. You can check these five variations by using the ABCs of interest payments. Although the U.S. government sets the maximum interest rates banks can pay on accounts under $100,000, not all banks pay the maximum. First you must find out if your bank pays the maximum rate of interest Allowed by law —the A of your "ABCDEs."

Second, find out what Balance (B of your "ABCDEs") your bank uses to figure this rate of interest. Banks use many different balances. If your bank figures interest on the smallest Balance in your account at the end of a quarter, this is to your least advantage; if your bank figures interest on the day-of-deposit to the day-of-withdrawal Balance, this is to your greatest advantage. For example, let's assume you have $1,000 in a savings account and you withdraw $950 just ten days before the end of a banking quarter (banking quarters are three-month periods usually ending March 31, June 30, September 30 and December 31). If interest is figured on the smallest Balance, you will receive interest on only $50 for that entire three-month period. However, if interest is figured on a day-of-deposit to day-of-withdrawal Balance, you will receive interest on $950 for three months less ten days plus interest on $50 for the entire three-month period. This amounts to quite a difference!

Third, check how often your interest is Compounded (C of your "ABCDEs"). Compounding interest means if you leave interest on deposit in your account, this interest will also earn additional interest. Naturally, the more often interest is Compounded the better. Daily Compounding of interest is to your greatest advantage.

Fourth, find out the number of Days of grace (D of your "ABCDEs") the bank allows. These are those Days before the end of a quarter when the bank allows you to withdraw your money and yet still pays you interest for that entire quarter; or those Days after the beginning of the quarter when the bank allows you to deposit your money and still pays you interest for that entire quarter. In other words, if a bank allows ten Days of grace at the beginning of every month, you can deposit your money up to the tenth of the month and still receive interest from the first Day of the month; that is, you will receive ten Days of free interest.

Last of all, find out how often your Earned interest (E of your "ABCDEs") is credited to your account—the oftener the better. The daily crediting of Earned interest would be the most to your advantage; however, most banks credit Earned interest quarterly.

The five ABCDE questions about interest payments are important to you because they determine if your savings earn the maximum or minimum amount of interest paid by banks. Therefore, let's take the time to review these questions.

A: asking your bank if it pays the maximum interest
rates Allowed by law.
B: asking your bank what Balance it uses to figure
your interest.
C: asking your bank how often it Compounds your
interest.
D: asking your bank what Days of grace it allows.
E: asking your bank how often your Earned interest is credited to your account.

Regular savings accounts, usually referred to as passbook savings accounts, seldom require a minimum deposit or notice for withdrawal. Because you can deposit or withdraw your money at any time without penalty, this account pays the least amount of interest—a maximum of 5% in 1975.

You can earn a higher rate of interest if you deposit $500 to $100,000 for a definite period of time ranging from ninety days to ten years. These savings accounts are called time deposits because you agree to leave your savings on "deposit" with the bank for a predetermined period of time. The longer the period, the more interest you will earn—from 5½% to 7½% in 1975. Time deposits are referred to by a variety of names such as golden passbook savings accounts, investment certificates or certificates of deposit (CDs).

In the 1970s, you would have earned the most interest if you deposited at least $100,000 for thirty days or longer in time deposits called certificates of deposit. Why? Because interest rates on savings accounts of $100,000 or more were not regulated by the U.S. government. Therefore, banks had no ceiling on the amount of interest these accounts can pay, and in 1974, CDs paid as much as 12¾% annual interest. CDs are generally not automatically renewed and stop earning interest at maturity.

You can borrow against all time deposits (use them as

collateral for a loan) at the bank where the time deposit is made. Federal rules require banks to charge interest rates of at least 2% more than the interest rate they pay you on a time deposit. Borrowing against time deposits is only profitable if the money is borrowed for a short time and if the time deposit has been in force a long time.

If you want to withdraw your money before a time deposit comes due, there is a penalty which is determined by federal rules (and which is standard for all banks). You lose three months' interest on the money withdrawn, and the interest paid reverts to the passbook savings rate (5% in 1975). However, this interest penalty can never reduce the amount of your original savings deposit. Time deposits (under $100,000) are usually renewed automatically if you do not redeem them within ten days after they come due.

Commercial banks are also offering retirement savings plans which qualify for the Individual Retirement Account (IRA) or the Keogh Plan (for details, see page 54). Find out the total interest paid (use your "ABCDEs"), the charges and the early withdrawal penalties on the retirement plans offered by commercial banks. Then compare what they offer with at least two competitive retirement plans (such as S&L retirement plans or U.S. retirement bonds).

How to Select a Maturity Date
Since time deposits mature anywhere from thirty days to ten years, how do you select a maturity date? If you need your cash repaid on a specific date, then that should be your maturity date. Why? Because the interest penalty for withdrawing money before a time deposit matures is much larger than the higher rate of interest you receive by choosing a longer maturity date.

However, if you will not need the money you are

depositing at any certain time, the future trend of interest rates should be your guideline. Although the U.S. government regulates interest rates on time deposits under $100,000, whenever interest rates on competitive investments get too far out of line, Uncle Sam will raise or lower the regulated interest rates. Therefore, if you expect interest rates to rise, you should select a short maturity date of four years or less in order to be able to reinvest your money at a higher rate of interest in a short time. On the other hand, if you expect interest rates to decline, you should select a longer maturity date in order to lock in a higher rate of interest for a longer time.

Now the big question is, How can you predict if interest rates are going to rise or decline? During inflationary times, people and businesses spend freely and borrow heavily, causing interest rates to rise. During deflationary times, people and businesses stop spending freely and borrowing heavily, causing interest rates to decline. In other words, when the demand for borrowing is greater, interest rates generally rise.

There are a few helpful guidelines to the future trend of interest rates. One is the weekly report by the Federal Reserve Bank of New York which states whether businesses are borrowing more or less at the twelve largest New York banks. The more businesses are borrowing, the more you can expect interest rates to rise; and the less businesses are borrowing, the more you can expect interest rates to decline. You can read this report as a news item every Friday in the *Wall Street Journal* or on the financial page of most city newspapers.

Another important indicator of the movement of interest rates is the prime rate. The prime rate is the rate of interest that the highest-quality corporations are charged when they borrow money from banks. In 1974 and 1975, for instance, the prime rate fluctuated between 7% and 12%. If you hear in the news that the prime rate has been raised, you can expect interest rates to increase, and if it has been lowered, you can expect interest rates to decrease.

How to Use a Commercial Bank to Your Advantage

To use a commercial bank to your advantage, first select one with a solid foundation and then keep only insured savings on deposit. If there are two or more equally safe banks to choose from, take into consideration the total yields they pay (using the ABCDE questions), what they charge for checking accounts and the services they offer that will save you time and money (such as bill-paying services, bookkeeping services or investment services). By selecting your bank carefully, you can give your savings more protection and more profitability.

Shirley Wrong Opens a Bank Account

As Shirley Wrong walks home from work, she notices the gala opening of a new branch of an established bank. When she finds out the bank is giving away a toaster with deposits of $1,000 or more, she opens a savings account and leaves the bank elated with her new toaster. Instead of finding out if the bank is likely to repay her savings immediately under all circumstances or if it pays the maximum allowed interest rates, she selected it for a bonus gift. This bank might not give her hard-earned money the necessary protection or profitability it deserves—*she is surely wrong.*

Shirley Wright Checks Her Bank for Safety and Profitability

Shirley Wright has banked at the same place for years and knows her savings are federally insured. When she realizes she has never checked the bank's annual statement, its interest rates or its convenient services, she

decides to do so. She calls her bank and finds out it is
a national bank with deposits of over $750 million. She
also requests its annual statement and is pleased to find
its loans are only 62% of its deposits, less than the suggested 70%.

She is also satisfied with the answers to the five
ABCDE questions—the bank pays the Allowable maximum interest rates, figures interest on a day-of-deposit
to day-of-withdrawal Balance, Compounds interest
daily, gives 10 Days of grace at the beginning of every
month and the Earned interest is credited quarterly. In
addition, the bank offers a combination savings-checking account which Shirley was not aware of. Now she
realizes it is up to her to keep up-to-date on the yields,
the types of accounts and the convenient services banks
offer—*she is surely right.*

The following charts give detailed information on savings accounts in commercial banks.

PASSBOOK SAVINGS ACCOUNTS—
COMMERCIAL BANKS

Type of Security

IOUs of commercial banks with passbooks issued in the owner's name.

Minimum Deposit

$5.

Yield (Maximum— 1975)

5% usually compounded daily and paid quarterly. An account closed before the quarter's end may lose interest for the entire quarter, which can be avoided by keeping $1 in the account until the quarter ends. Savings deposited during the first 10 days of January, April, July and October usually receive interest from the first day even if deposited as late as the 10th day.

Safety

The repayment of the savings deposit as well as the payment of interest is guaranteed by the bank and up to $40,000 may be guaranteed by a federal corporation—the FDIC.

How Much Liquidity?

Savings can normally be withdrawn at any time, but banks can require depositors to give a 30-day written notice of intent to withdraw savings.

TIME DEPOSIT ACCOUNTS—
COMMERCIAL BANKS
($500 to $99,999*)
(Also referred to as golden passbook
accounts, investment certificates, term
deposits and certificates of deposit)

Type of Security

IOUs of commercial banks
that pay different rates of
interest for different maturity
dates. Receipts are certificates
or passbooks issued in the
owner's name.

Minimum Deposit

$500 to $1,000.

Maturity Dates and
Yields (Maximum—
1975)

Interest on time deposits is
usually compounded
quarterly and paid quarterly
or at maturity for 90 days to
1 year: 5½%; 1 to 2½ years:
6%; 2½ to 4 years: 6½%; 4
to 6 years: 7¼%; 6 to 10
years: 7½%.

Safety

The repayment of time
deposits as well as the
payment of interest is
guaranteed by the bank and
up to $40,000 may be
guaranteed by a federal
corporation—the FDIC.

How Much Liquidity?

Although time deposits can normally be cashed at any time, banks can require depositors to give a 30-day written notice of intent to withdraw savings. In addition, time deposits cashed before maturity forfeit 3 months' interest on the amount withdrawn, and the interest paid is reduced to the passbook savings rate. Also, banks will loan money on their time deposits and charge at least 2% above the interest rate paid by the time deposits.

*Certificates of deposit of $100,000 or more are also sold but their interest rates are not regulated by the U.S. government.

SAVINGS AND LOAN ASSOCIATIONS
(S&Ls)

In the 1970s, S&Ls (sometimes called building and loan associations, homestead associations or cooperative banks) were constantly advertising that they pay the highest rate of interest on federally insured savings accounts. The reason for this is that S&Ls are required by law to reloan their savings deposits primarily for home mortgages. In order to attract more money for home mortgages, the U.S. government allows S&Ls to pay slightly higher rates of interest than commercial banks.

Why You Must Be Careful Choosing S&Ls
Since S&Ls loan your savings (which you deposit for months or a few years) for mortgages (which are not repaid for twenty or thirty years), the cash position of S&Ls can be susceptible to strain. S&Ls are allowed by law to loan up to 94% of their savings deposits in long-term property mortgages. Therefore, they may have as little as 6% in liquid assets. In addition, most S&Ls by law can offer only savings accounts (not checking accounts or full banking services). Thus, they attract savings solely because they pay slightly higher interest rates. When S&L interest rates are not competitive with other interest-paying investments, savers make large withdrawals to earn higher interest rates elsewhere. This also drains S&L cash reserves. For example, in a period of just 1 month (August, 1974) when the U.S. Treasury sold $1,000 Treasury notes paying 9% annual interest, depositors withdrew over $1 billion of savings from S&Ls in order to buy these higher-yielding investments. As a result, the Treasury temporarily raised the minimum price for Treasury notes from $1,000 to $5,000, a price too high for the small investor.

The cash position of a S&L may have an effect on whether or not that S&L is able to repay your savings immediately. That is why it is necessary to choose your S&L carefully.

Choosing Your S&L

Well-managed, large S&Ls (with deposits of $500 million or more) that are members of the Federal Home Loan Bank System and members of the Federal Savings and Loan Insurance Corporation (FSLIC) are more likely to repay your savings under all circumstances. Here's why. Well-managed S&Ls have a history of profitable operations; thus they are better prepared to cope with new problems. Large S&Ls usually offer more financial strength than smaller S&Ls. Furthermore, S&Ls that are members of the Federal Home Loan Bank System are examined regularly by its Board and can borrow money from Federal Home Loan Banks if ever necessary. In addition, S&Ls that are members of the FSLIC offer federally insured bank accounts. Members of the FSLIC pay deposit insurance annually, and should a S&L fail, the FSLIC promises to repay individual depositors up to a $40,000 limit on each account.

The FSLIC is a self-supporting federal corporation with limited borrowing privileges from the U.S. Treasury. Therefore, a guarantee by the FSLIC is not a guarantee by the U.S. government. The FSLIC offers approximately the same protection as the FDIC (see page 10).

S&Ls, like commercial banks, have the right to require a thirty-day written notice before you can withdraw money from your savings account. Although this right has not been used since 1935, it exists and can be enforced if ever necessary (for more details, see page 10).

Some S&Ls also have an additional right that com-

mercial banks do not have. S&Ls that do not have cash
to repay your withdrawal request after the thirty-day
period can use the rotation system. The rotation system
allows the S&L to repay withdrawal requests up to the
amount of $1,000 in the order they are received. Thus,
if your request is $2,000, you are paid only $1,000 the
first time, and then your request goes to the bottom of
the list and you wait your turn to receive your second
$1,000. If S&L supervisors think the S&L can eventu-
ally straighten out its own affairs, the rotation plan can
continue and the FSLIC is not legally required to step
in and pay off depositors.

From 1935 to 1975, the FSLIC has taken over as soon
as one S&L depositor was not repaid, and it also repaid
all insured deposits immediately. Nevertheless, techni-
cally speaking, most S&Ls have the right to use the
rotation system and during past financial crises, the rotation system has been used.

As with commercial banks (see page 11), it is a good
idea to check the percentage of deposits S&Ls have in
loans. You will probably find that most S&Ls have more
than 70% of their deposits in loans. In exchange for
giving up the maximum liquidity you require of commercial banks, you will receive slightly higher interest
rates from S&Ls.

How can you locate well-managed, large S&Ls that
are members of the Federal Home Loan Bank System
and members of the FSLIC? Any local S&L will give
you the address and telephone number of the nearest
Federal Home Loan Bank, which in turn will give you
the names of the S&Ls you are looking for. You can
request an annual report from each S&L. Then check
in the annual report for the percentage of its deposits
in loans as well as its record of profits for the past several
years. This will reflect how well the S&L has been
managed.

Types of S&L Bank Accounts

A few S&Ls in eastern states are authorized by law to offer checking accounts and many of the remaining S&Ls are making arrangements with commercial banks so that their depositors can receive free checking accounts or pay reduced charges for checking accounts.

S&L savings plans are similar to commercial bank savings plans except their rates of interest on deposits under $100,000 are ¼% to ½% more annually as allowed by law (for more details, see page 12). Interest rates on S&L CDs over $100,000 are not regulated by law and generally pay the same rate of interest as commercial bank CDs. You should check S&L savings plans to see whether they pay you the maximum amount of interest by finding the answers to the five ABC questions (see pages 12–15 for details).

You can borrow on S&L savings plans just as you would borrow on commercial bank savings plans. Federal regulations require S&Ls to charge you at least 1% more than the rate of interest their time deposits pay. Borrowing against time deposits is only profitable if the money is borrowed for a short time and if the time deposit has been in force a long time.

You can also withdraw your money from S&L time deposits before they come due. Federal rules require S&Ls to charge the same large interest penalty for early withdrawal as commercial banks charge—loss of three months' interest on the amount you withdraw and interest paid reverts to the passbook savings rate.

S&Ls, like commercial banks, offer retirement savings plans which qualify for the Individual Retirement Plan as well as for the Keogh Plan (for details, see page 54). Find out the total interest the S&L retirement plans pay (using your five ABC questions) as well as their charges and early withdrawal penalties. Then compare them with at least two competitive retire-

ment plans (such as commercial bank retirement plans
or U.S. retirement bonds).

How to Use S&Ls to Your Advantage
Select a S&L more likely to repay your savings under
all circumstances and then keep only insured savings
on deposit. If there are two or more such S&Ls to
choose from, take into consideration the total interest
they pay (using your ABC questions to check), what
arrangements and charges they make for checking accounts and what free services they offer that will save
you time and money (such as safety deposit boxes, trav-
elers checks and notary service). If you give your savings additional protection and more profitability, you
are using S&Ls to your advantage.

Where Should Shirley Wright Deposit Her Savings?
Shirley Wright has a combination savings-checking account in her commercial bank. Now she wants to compare this account with a S&L savings account to determine which is more to her advantage.

Shirley knows commercial banks offer her full banking services, whereas most S&Ls offer only savings accounts. In addition, Shirley knows her bank has only
62% of its deposits in loans, whereas all the S&Ls she
checked had over 85% of their deposits in loans. On the
other hand, S&Ls offer many free services as well as
slightly higher interest rates. But how much more interest does the S&L pay and what does this mean in
actual money to her? S&Ls pay ¼% to ½% more annually on their savings plans than commercial banks
which means $2.50 or $5 more a year to her on her
$1,000 savings deposit.

Both S&Ls and commercial banks charge the same
large interest penalty if savings are withdrawn before
a time deposit comes due. In addition, both S&Ls and
commercial banks allow her to borrow money on a time

deposit rather than paying the large interest penalty. In case Shirley ever decides to borrow, federal rules allow S&Ls to charge her 1% less annual interest than commercial banks are allowed to charge for the loan on a time deposit.

After completing this comparison, Shirley decides to give up the small interest benefits and the free services offered by S&Ls for her commercial bank's larger percentage of liquid assets and for the convenience of full-service banking all in one place.

Shirley's brother, on the other hand, makes the same comparison and decides to deposit his savings in a S&L savings account. He feels the S&L he has selected is likely to repay his savings under all circumstances. Although this S&L had over 85% of its deposits in loans, he realizes they may be able to sell mortgages, if ever necessary, to raise additional cash. He also prefers the slightly higher interest rates and the other free services S&Ls offer. Furthermore, this S&L made it possible for him to get a mortgage in order to buy his house.

After considering her brother's choice, Shirley comes to the conclusion that investing is a personal decision and different people have different comfort zones. That is why the same investment does not fit everybody's needs—*she is surely right.*

Make your own comparison and come to your own conclusion. The following charts give information on the various S&L accounts. This information can be used for choosing savings accounts as well as for comparing these accounts with other investments.

TIME DEPOSIT ACCOUNTS—SAVINGS AND LOAN ASSOCIATIONS (S&Ls)
($500 to $99,000*)
(Also referred to as golden passbook accounts, investment certificates, term deposits and certificates of deposit)

Type of Security

IOUs of S&Ls or shareholder accounts that pay different rates of interest for different maturity dates. Receipts are certificates or passbooks issued in the owner's name.

Minimum Deposit

$500 to $1,000.

Maturity Dates and Yields (Maximum—1975)

Interest on time deposits is usually compounded daily and paid quarterly or at maturity for 90 days to 1 year: 5¾%; 1 to 2½ years: 6½%; 2½ to 4 years: 6¾%; 4 to 6 years: 7½%; 6 to 10 years: 7¾%.

Safety

The repayment of time deposits as well as the payment of interest is guaranteed by the S&L and up to $40,000 may be guaranteed by a federal corporation—the FSLIC.

How Much
Liquidity?

Although time deposits can
normally be cashed at any
time, S&Ls can require
depositors to give a 30-day
written notice of intent to
withdraw savings. In addition,
time deposits cashed before
maturity forfeit 3 months'
interest on the amount
withdrawn, and the interest
paid is reduced to the
passbook savings rate. Also,
S&Ls will loan money on
their time deposits and
charge at least 1% above the
interest rates paid by the
time deposits.

*Certificates of deposit of $100,000 or more are sold but their
interest rates are not regulated by the U.S. government.

PASSBOOK SAVINGS ACCOUNTS—
SAVINGS & LOAN ASSOCIATIONS (S&Ls)

Type of Security

IOUs of S&Ls or shareholder accounts with passbooks issued in the owner's name.

Minimum Deposit

$5.

Yield (Maximum—1975)

5¼% usually compounded daily and paid quarterly. An account closed before the quarter's end usually loses interest for that entire quarter, which can be avoided by keeping $1 in the account until the quarter ends. Savings deposited during the first 10 days of January, April, July and October usually receive interest from the first day of the month even if deposited as late as the 10th day.

Safety

The repayment of the savings deposit as well as the payment of interest is guaranteed by the S&L and up to $40,000 may be guaranteed by the FSLIC.

How Much Liquidity?

Savings can normally be withdrawn at any time, but S&Ls can require depositors to give a 30-day written notice of intent to withdraw savings.

SWISS BANKS

For years, people from all over the world have deposited money in Swiss banks. Why are Swiss banks so special? They are safe, but so are many other banks. The reason for the popularity of Swiss banks is that they offer privacy to depositors. Swiss banks have confidential numbered accounts, and there is no way for anyone to check the depositors' identities. Furthermore, even accounts that bear depositors' names have almost complete privacy in Switzerland. The privacy of a Swiss bank account can be invaded only if the money deposited was acquired through acts considered crimes by Swiss law, for example, kidnapping, robbery, drug trade and extortion. Since many foreigners open Swiss bank accounts to evade their national income tax, to own gold and to keep money outside their native country, which are not crimes under Swiss law, their privacy cannot be invaded.

In the 1970s, another reason contributed to the popularity of Swiss bank accounts. Americans wanted to convert some of their U.S. dollars to Swiss francs. Why? Because dollars were losing value in relation to Swiss francs. From 1971 to 1975, the value of the Swiss franc increased 80% from 23¢ to 41¢. An investment of $500 in Swiss francs deposited in a Swiss bank account would have doubled in four years—an 80% gain in the value of the Swiss franc plus 20% earned in interest (5% for each of the four years). Of course, at other times, the Swiss franc can lose in value in relation to the dollar. Thus, when you see the U.S. government halt its deficit spending and develop a favorable balance of trade, you should convert Swiss francs back into dollars.

Swiss banks will convert Swiss francs into dollars at any time. As a matter of fact, they offer accounts in

many foreign currencies. These accounts can also be
used to buy stocks, bonds, currencies, silver, gold and
many investments anywhere in the world.

Choosing a Swiss Bank
Unless you have the ability to analyze banks, it is safer
to limit your choice to the three big banks in Switzerland: Swiss Bank Corporation, Swiss Credit Bank or
Union Bank of Switzerland. It is unlikely that these
three big Swiss banks will ever be in financial trouble.
If they are, however, the Swiss government would
probably come to their aid because banking is Switzerland's life blood. Although there are convenient
branches of these Swiss banks in the United States, they
are regulated by American banking laws and also do
not offer you the privacy of a Swiss bank account
opened in Switzerland.

Opening a Swiss Bank Account
Swiss banks generally offer interest-paying accounts in
dollars, French francs, English pounds, German marks
and most major foreign currencies. These are time
deposits that come due in thirty days to one year and
are renewable. Although you are generally required to
deposit a minimum of about $25,000, you are not re-
stricted by any maximum amount. The interest rates on
these accounts are determined at the time of deposit.
(Use your ABC questions, see pages 12–15).

Swiss banks also offer interest-paying accounts and
non-interest-paying accounts in Swiss francs. You are
usually required to deposit a minimum of about $500.
Also, as of October, 1974, foreigners were limited to
depositing a total of 100,000 Swiss francs, of which only
50,000 Swiss francs could be deposited in an interest-
paying account, and 50,000 Swiss francs could be
deposited in a non-interest-paying account. On deposits over 100,000 Swiss francs, foreigners were charged

a large penalty. They must pay interest to the Swiss bank of 10% a quarter, or 40% a year, for the privilege of depositing more than 100,000 Swiss francs. At that time the Swiss franc was worth 35¢, so a deposit of 100,000 Swiss francs was worth $35,000.

Why was this restriction placed on foreigners? In 1974, the Swiss franc was gaining in value in relation to most other foreign currencies. As a result, foreigners began converting staggering amounts of their weaker currencies into stronger Swiss francs and depositing them in Swiss bank accounts. Thus the Swiss government put a limit on the amount each person could deposit. However, this limitation will probably be removed as soon as the Swiss franc is no longer subject to heavy speculation.

Swiss banks offer several types of Swiss franc interest-paying accounts, all of which have strict withdrawal restrictions. Although you can withdraw all the Swiss francs you deposit in interest-paying accounts if you notify the bank three to six months before you want your money, these accounts limit the amount of Swiss francs you can withdraw without prior notice. For example, private accounts (sometimes called cash deposit accounts) paying up to 3½% annual interest limit withdrawals to 10,000 Swiss francs a month without prior notice; savings accounts paying up to 5% interest limit withdrawals to 5,000 Swiss francs a month without prior notice; and investment savings accounts paying up to 5½% interest usually limit withdrawals to 3,000 Swiss francs a month without prior notice. Thus, the more Swiss francs you are allowed to withdraw without prior notice, the less interest you receive.

This information about the reasons for owning a Swiss bank account as well as the different accounts that are offered will help you determine the value of a Swiss bank account in your investment program. Ask yourself these questions: Is there a reason for you to have $500

or more deposited in a bank outside of the United
States? Do you need complete banking privacy? Do you
feel comfortable with money in a currency other than
the U.S. dollar? Is this the time when the Swiss franc
may be appreciating in value in relation to the dollar?
Do Swiss banks pay more interest than U.S. banks? The
answers to these questions will help you judge your
need for a Swiss bank account.

If you decide to open a Swiss bank account, you can
write a letter stating the type of account as well as the
currency for the account, where the correspondence
should be mailed (request correspondence in English),
and the names of the account holders. (You can avoid
administrative problems in the event of death by opening foreign bank accounts in at least two names—joint
tenancy with the right of survivorship.) Then mail the
letter with a bank cashier's check (personal checks are
usually not acceptable) made payable to one of the
three large banks in Switzerland:

Swiss Bank Corporation
Paradeplatz 6
8022 Zurich, Switzerland, Europe

Swiss Credit Bank
Paradeplatz 6
8022 Zurich, Switzerland, Europe

Union Bank of Switzerland
Bahnhofstrasse 45
8021 Zurich, Switzerland, Europe

Disadvantages of a Swiss Bank Account
Having a bank account thousands of miles away is a
disadvantage for several reasons. Correspondence by
mail takes longer and is more troublesome. It takes
time to become familiar with the different types of
Swiss bank accounts. Also, Swiss bank statements can be

confusing; for example, they use periods where you use commas and commas where you use periods, so your balance would read 10.000 Swiss francs instead of 10,-000 Swiss francs.

In addition, as of January, 1976, Swiss banks automatically deduct a 35% Swiss federal withholding tax on interest, and although U.S. citizens are entitled to a 30% refund, this refund is a nuisance to get back. You request an R-82 form from a Swiss bank which you complete and send to the Swiss government (be sure to ask for all correspondence in English). Then, after several months of perseverance and a lot of paper work, you do receive the 30% refund. The other 5% can be used as a tax credit against your federal income tax, though separate forms must be attached to your income tax return to claim this tax credit.

Many of these disadvantages can be overcome with time, patience and the familiarity of doing business with a Swiss bank.

Shirley Wrong's Letter to Open a Swiss Bank Account

September 1, 1974

Dear Sir:

Enclosed is my personal check for $500. Would you kindly open a Swiss bank account for me.

Sincerely,
Ms. Shirley Wrong
1 Cumbersome Way
Confusion City, Nevada 89701 USA

Shirley Wrong's personal check is returned with a letter written in French. After an exchange of several letters, she finally opens her Swiss franc bank account on November 1. Since Shirley Wrong sends a personal check instead of a bank cashier's check, does not state the type of interest-paying Swiss franc account she wants and does not ask for her correspondence in English, she wastes time and money—*she is surely wrong.*

Shirley Wright's Letter to Open a Swiss Bank Account

September 1, 1974

Dear Sir:

Enclosed is a cashier's check for $5,000. Would you convert my dollars to Swiss francs and open an interest-paying investment savings account in Swiss francs paying 5½% annual interest in the names of Ms. Shirley Wright and Mr. I. M. Wright (in joint tenancy with right of survivorship). Please send all correspondence in English to 1 Efficient Place, Knowledge City, California 90230, U.S.A. Also, mail the interest to me in U.S. dollars whenever it is paid.* I would also appreciate an R-82 form mailed to me with each interest check. Thanking you in advance.

Sincerely,
Ms. Shirley Wright

Shirley receives a letter from the Swiss bank welcoming her as a depositor and asking her to put her account number, 57–127, at the top of all future correspondence. There were also two enclosures: a signature card which has to be signed and verified by a large American bank and a credit slip (or credit advice) for 17.000 Swiss francs. Shirley divides her 17.000 Swiss francs by $5,000 (their cost); this determines that the price she has paid for each Swiss franc is 34¢.

---

*Some investors prefer to have the interest earned accumulate in Swiss francs in their savings accounts.

In April, Shirley notices in the *Wall Street Journal* (under Foreign Exchange) that the price of a Swiss franc has increased to 40¢. In just seven months, the Swiss franc has gained in value by more than 17% in relation to the dollar. She decides to withdraw and convert 3,000 Swiss francs into dollars (the number of Swiss francs she can withdraw from her investment savings account without prior notice). The price of the Swiss franc may go up or down before her letter reaches Switzerland, but the change will probably be very little. Shirley writes the following letter:

April 10, 1975

57–127

Dear Sir:

Would you kindly withdraw 3,000 Swiss francs from account 57–127 and convert them into U.S. dollars. Then send me a check payable in dollars for this amount as soon as possible. Thanking you in advance.

Sincerely,
Ms. Shirley Wright
1 Efficient Way
Knowledge City, Calif. 90230 USA

Three weeks later, Shirley receives a debit advice for 3,000 Swiss francs and a check for $1,205, which is $185 more than she originally paid seven months before for these 3,000 Swiss francs. Because she has owned the Swiss francs longer than six months, her $185 profit is a capital gain, which is usually taxed at one-half the ordinary income tax rate—*she is surely right.*

The following charts give you detailed information on the 1975 status of the most common Swiss franc interest-paying accounts. These accounts vary slightly at the three large Swiss banks and may change from time to time.

DEPOSIT ACCOUNTS IN SWISS FRANCS
(Also called cash deposit or private accounts)

Type of Security	IOUs of a Swiss bank. Receipts are generally credit advices and annual statements.
Minimum Deposit (1975)	Usually $500.
Maximum Deposit (1975) paying interest	50,000 Swiss francs (for foreigners).
Yield (Maximum— 1975)	3½%, which is paid at the end of the year (or at withdrawal). Interest is subject to a 35% Swiss federal withholding tax, 30% of which is refundable to U.S. citizens and the other 5% can be used as a tax credit against U.S. income tax.
Safety	The repayment of the savings deposit and the payment of interest are guaranteed by the Swiss bank.
How Much Liquidity?	Up to 10,000 Swiss francs can be withdrawn a month without notice; for larger amounts, 3 months' notice is usually required.

SAVINGS ACCOUNTS IN SWISS FRANCS

Type of Security	IOUs of a Swiss bank. Receipts are generally credit advices and annual statements.
Minimum Deposit (1975)	Usually $500.
Maximum Deposit (1975) paying interest	50,000 Swiss francs (for foreigners).
Yield (Maximum—1975)	5%, which is paid at the end of the year (or at withdrawal). Interest is subject to a 35% Swiss federal withholding tax, 30% of which is refundable to U.S. citizens and the other 5% can be used as a tax credit against U.S. income tax.
Safety	The repayment of the savings deposit and the payment of interest are guaranteed by the Swiss bank. Also, under the Swiss banking act, the first 5,000 Swiss francs have extra protection.
How Much Liquidity?	Up to 5,000 Swiss francs can be withdrawn a month without notice; for larger amounts, 6 months' notice is usually required.

INVESTMENT SAVINGS ACCOUNTS IN SWISS FRANCS

Type of Security

IOUs of Swiss banks. Receipts are generally credit advices and annual statements.

Minimum Deposit (1975) paying interest

Usually $500.

Maximum Deposit (1975)

50,000 Swiss francs (for foreigners).

Yield (Maximum— 1975)

6%, which is usually paid at the end of the year (or at withdrawal). Interest is subject to a 35% Swiss federal withholding tax, 30% of which is refundable to U.S. citizens and the other 5% can be used as a tax credit against U.S. income tax.

Safety

The repayment of a savings deposit and the payment of interest are guaranteed by the Swiss bank.

How Much Liquidity?

Up to 3,000 or 5,000 Swiss francs can be withdrawn per calendar half year without notice; for larger amounts, 6 months' notice is usually required.

Should You Loan Your Money to the U.S. Government by Purchasing U.S. Savings Bonds? U.S. Retirement Bonds? Treasury Securities?

Uncle Sam sells U.S. government securities to raise billions of dollars to finance his spending programs. But exactly what are U.S. government securities? They are time deposits, just like those in banks. You deposit your savings with the U.S. government for specific periods of time by purchasing U.S. savings bonds, U.S. retirement bonds and Treasury securities. In other words, rather than loaning your money to a bank, you are loaning your money to the U.S. government, which pays you interest for the use of your money and repays your savings deposit when the securities come due.

Instead of receiving a bankbook as a receipt for your savings deposit with the U.S. government, you receive a certificate. This certificate cannot be increased in value by depositing more money, in the way a bank account is increased. So, if you want to deposit more money, you must buy additional government securities for which you will receive additional certificates. Each certificate has a dollar value printed on its face. This face value (often called par) is the amount of money Uncle Sam pays you when your U.S. government securities come due.

Since government securities are guaranteed by the full faith and credit of the U.S. government, they offer unequaled safety. If ever necessary, the Treasury can print money to repay you. Furthermore, their interest is exempt from state and local income taxes and they usually pay higher interest rates than savings accounts. It's no wonder that government securities are the backbone of the investment program of most banks and financial institutions. You should consider making them the backbone of your investment program, too.

U.S. SAVINGS BONDS

You are probably familiar with U.S. savings bonds, although you may not be aware of the many advantages they offer you. Savings bonds are U.S. government time deposits, but they have different rules from bank time deposits. You can cash savings bonds any time after the first few months without paying a penalty; whereas if you cash bank time deposits before they come due, you always pay a large interest penalty. Furthermore, the rate of interest savings bonds pay is graduated and increases every six months up until their original maturity date, whereas bank time deposits pay the same rate of interest to maturity. In addition, if you do not cash savings bonds, they are automatically renewed and interest continues for at least ten years beyond their original maturity. Savings bonds that are automatically renewed pay interest on a new graduated cycle, and you receive the same rate of interest as you would had you bought new savings bonds on that same day. Since the rate of interest paid by savings bonds has been raised continually from 1935 to 1975, they offer some inflation hedge to the small investor with as little as $18.75 to invest.

In 1975, savings bonds paid a yield of 6% if they were held to maturity. This interest is worth even more than 6% because it is exempt from state and local income taxes. You can also receive a month's free interest if you purchase savings bonds at the end of the month. Why? Because they are dated and pay interest from the first day of the month even if they are purchased on the last day. However, if you cash a savings bond on a date other than the one on the certificate or six months from that date, you will lose interest because a savings bond pays interest only at six-month intervals.

You can buy savings bonds at commercial banks (and sometimes at S&Ls and mutual savings banks) or at Federal Reserve Banks without paying a purchase or redemption charge. In addition, you can arrange regular monthly purchases through payroll savings plans where you work or through the Bond-A-Month Plan where you bank.

If savings bonds are lost or stolen, the U.S. government will replace them without a charge. One restriction is that you cannot sell your Savings bonds to other investors and you cannot borrow against them (use them as collateral for a loan). Furthermore, the government only allows you to buy face amounts of $10,000 every calendar year in each of the two types of savings bonds—Series E and Series H bonds.

E Bonds

Series E bonds are five-year time deposits which sell
for a variety of prices starting at $18.75. If you pay
$18.75 for an E bond, the U.S. Treasury will pay you
$25.20 in five years. The difference between the
$18.75 purchase price and the $25.20 redemption
price is your interest, which is paid only when you
cash E bonds. In the meantime, E bonds appreciate
in value every six months by the amount of interest
that is accumulating. In 1975, E bonds paid a graduated rate of interest starting at 4.54% the first year
and increasing every six months so that E bonds held
to maturity averaged 6% annually.

Although E bond interest is not subject to state or
local income taxes, it is subject to federal income tax.
This interest does not have to be reported as it accumulates annually; instead, you can postpone the reporting
of your interest until E bonds are cashed (which can be
months to fifteen years or longer). This income tax postponement can be a valuable tax benefit because you
can buy E bonds during your working years when you
are in a high tax bracket and then cash them during
your retirement years when you will be in a lower tax
bracket. The 6% annual interest of E bonds if held to
maturity can be worth as much as 8% when tax advantages are taken into consideration—the exemption
from state and local income taxes as well as the postponement of federal income tax. If you have E bonds
with redemption values of at least $500, you can ex-
change them for H bonds. The advantage of this is that
you will receive your interest twice a year instead of
having it accumulate until your E bonds are cashed.
Although you will pay federal income tax on H bonds'
current income, you can continue to postpone federal
income tax on the interest accumulated on the E bonds
you exchanged until the H bonds are cashed.

E bonds are useful as a tax-free education plan for your children. You can purchase them in a child's name with an adult as beneficiary (not co-owner). To show your intent, you may file a federal income tax return in the child's name reporting the amount of interest that has accumulated on the E bonds the first year (no matter how small). You can find out the amount of this interest at your bank. Then, all E bond interest that accumulates is 100% tax-free as long as the child does not earn more than $1,750 a year, which includes the $1,000 standard income tax deduction. If you invested $75 in E bonds every month for fifteen years (at the same rate of interest they paid in 1975), the child would accumulate $21,397 of E bonds, and of this total, $7,117 will be tax-free interest.

The *E* in *E* bonds should remind you that they are for *E*verybody because they are inexpensive, lend themselves to regular weekly or monthly savings plans and offer tax benefits.

H Bonds

Series H bonds are ten-year time deposits which sell for $500, $1,000, $5,000 or $10,000. If you pay $500 for an H bond, the government repays you $500 at maturity. Why? Because H bond interest does not accumulate. Instead, you receive an interest check from the government every six months. H bonds can be cashed any time after the first six months for their original cost except during the month preceding an interest payment because interest checks for that six-month period are already being processed by the Treasury.

In 1975, the rate of interest paid by H bonds was on a graduated scale starting at 4.99% for the first year and increasing every six months to average 6% if held to maturity. H bonds not redeemed at maturity are automatically renewed, and the graduated interest cycle starts again with the second ten years. The *H* in *H*

bonds should remind you of the *H*andy current income
they pay twice a year.

How to Use Savings Bonds to Your Advantage
Before you buy savings bonds, determine if they fit
your investment needs by considering their six essential investment ingredients, which apply to all other
investments as well. These six essentials will be easy to
remember because their first initials spell the two
words MY CASH.

*M—M*aturity date, or the date on which an investment comes due and is repaid. Check for an early
withdrawal penalty should you want cash before
the investment matures.

*Y—Y*ield, or the total amount of annual interest or
dividend income an investment pays. This amount
is reduced by a purchase or redemption charge
and is increased by interest benefits and tax benefits. You can only compare the yields of investments with similar maturity dates, referred to as
"like" investments because similar investments
pay the same yields only when they have similar maturity dates, whereas similar investments do not pay the same yields for different
maturity dates. Usually, the longer the time to maturity, the higher the yield. For example, in 1975,
a bank time deposit coming due in up to one year
paid up to 5¾% annual interest, whereas one coming due in six to ten years paid up to 7¾% annual
interest.

*C—C*all provision, or a provision which allows the
issuer to shorten the maturity date by repaying an
investment before it comes due. For example,
Treasury bonds (see page 66) are sometimes issued
with a call provision which allows the government
to repay their face value five years before they

come due even if the owners do not want their bonds cashed.

A—*A*nticipated profit or loss, or when an investment can be sold for more or less than its original cost.

S—*S*afety, or who guarantees an investment including their credit rating, the length of time they have been in business and the history of their past uninterrupted interest or dividend payments.

H—*H*ow much liquidity, or how much cash you can get from an investment at a moment's notice. Liquidity is reduced if there is a selling charge or an early withdrawal penalty. Liquidity is important because emergencies arise when you need cash immediately.

After you have checked the six investment essentials to determine if savings bonds meet your investment needs, then you should shop investments—the same way you shop for anything else. You compare savings bonds with other "like" investments available in your price range and buy the best value at that time. How do you compare investments? You compare the investments on each of the six ingredients that make up the MY CASH checklist. This information will help you use savings bonds (as well as all other investments) to your advantage.

Shirley Wrong Decides Not to Use the MY CASH Checklist

Shirley Wrong has $1,000 to invest. She reads a newspaper ad stating that six-year time deposits of $1,000 or more earn 8.06% in a federally insured S&L account. Since 8.06% annual interest is much more than the 6% interest that savings bonds pay, Shirley decides there is no need to use the MY CASH checklist. She immediately deposits her $1,000 in a S&L time deposit. She does not want to lose one day's interest.

Six months later, Shirley needs her $1,000. When she withdraws her savings, she receives only $14.68 interest, half as much interest as savings bonds or S&L time deposits maturing in six months would pay. Since she did not use the MY CASH checklist, she did not realize there is a large early withdrawal interest penalty. Not only does the early withdrawal penalty reduce the 8.-06% interest to 5¼%, but she loses three months' interest as well—*she is surely wrong.*

Shirley Wright Uses the MY CASH Checklist to Compare Investments

Shirley Wright has $1,000 to invest. She wants to know if savings bonds or commercial bank time deposits are the better buy at that time. She uses the MY CASH checklist to compare the two investments.

Since there is a possibility she may need her money in six months, she selects a six-month *M*aturity date. Both savings bonds and three-month commercial bank time deposits allow her to withdraw money at the end of six months without penalty.

Next, Shirley compares the *Y*ields. She calls her commercial bank and finds out that E bonds held for six months will pay 3.73% annually and H bonds will pay 4.2%. Naturally, she prefers $1,000 worth of H bonds, which she figures will pay $21 interest for six months. This interest is increased to $27 when she includes the value of the tax benefit and a month's free interest (it is the end of the month and H bonds are dated and pay interest from the first day of the month).

Then Shirley asks the bank about time deposits. She finds out that three-month to one-year time deposits all pay 5½% interest. She prefers a $1,000 three-month time deposit because earned interest is then credited to her account at the end of the three months and compounds the second three months. In other words, the

first three months she has $1,000 in her time deposit
account, which earns $13.75. The second three months,
she has $1013.75 in her bank time deposit account, so
she earns more interest—$14.14. This gives her a total
of $27.69 for the six months.

Neither savings bonds nor bank time deposits have
Call provisions. Furthermore, they cannot be sold to
other investors, so there can never be an Anticipated
profit or a loss. So Shirley goes right on to Safety. Savings bonds are safer because they are directly guaranteed by the U.S. government, whereas bank time
deposits are guaranteed by a self-supporting federal
corporation (FDIC or FSLIC) with limited borrowing
privileges from the U.S. Treasury.

And now for H—How much liquidity. The U.S. government will cash H bonds immediately and normally
the bank will also cash time deposits in six months.
However, if ever necessary, a bank can require a thirty-
day written withdrawal request before giving cash for
time deposits.

After using the MY CASH checklist, it is obvious to
Shirley that she would rather buy H bonds than a bank
time deposit. Although H bonds pay less interest for six
months, they give her a combination of more safety and
more liquidity. Shirley buys two $500 H bonds by filling
out H bond applications at her bank. The bank forwards
her application to the Federal Reserve Bank and several weeks later Shirley receives her H bonds registered in her name—*she is surely right.*

The following individual accounts of E bonds and H
bonds may be helpful when you want to buy savings
bonds or when you want to compare them with other
investments.

U.S. SAVINGS BONDS—SERIES E*

Type of Security	IOUs of the U.S. government —registered certificates.
Purchase Prices Redemption Prices at Maturity (1975)	$18.75 $37.50 $56.25 $75.00 $25.20 $50.40 $75.60 $100.80
Purchase Prices Redemption Prices at Maturity (1975)	$150.00 $375 $750 $201.60 $504 $1,008
Where to Buy and Redeem	Purchases limited to $10,000 per person annually (redemption prices). They can be bought and cashed at Federal Reserve Banks, at most commercial banks and at S&Ls and mutual savings banks that qualify (no charge).
Maturity Date	5 years and can be retained at least an additional 10 years with interest continuing at the current E bond interest rate.
Yield (Maximum— 1975)	6% compounded semiannually if held to maturity. This interest is graduated starting at 4.54% the first year and increasing every 6 months for 5 years. However, interest is only paid when E bonds are cashed. Interest is exempt from state

and local income taxes, and federal income tax can be postponed until E bonds are cashed. Bonds cashed before a 6-month interval lose interest. Bonds purchased during the month are dated and pay interest from the first day of the month.

*C*all Provision	Not callable.
*A*nticipated Profit or Loss (other than interest income)	No anticipated profit or loss because they cannot be sold to other investors.
*S*afety	The repayment of their purchase price as well as the payment of interest is guaranteed by the U.S. government.
*H*ow Much Liquidity?	Bonds can be cashed any time after the first 2 months; however, no interest is paid if cashed before 6 months. They cannot be borrowed against.

*Bicentennial savings bonds were sold between May 1, 1975, and December 31, 1976, with the same characteristics as regular savings bonds.

U.S. SAVINGS BONDS—SERIES H

Type of Security	IOUs of the U.S. government —registered certificates.
Face of Par Value (Redemption Prices)	$500, $1,000, $5,000, $10,000.
Where to Buy and Redeem	H bond purchases are limited to $10,000 per person annually. They can be bought and cashed at Federal Reserve Banks (no charge). Many commercial banks will forward applications to buy or to cash H bonds to Federal Reserve Banks (no charge).
Maturity Date	10 years (can be retained at least an additional 10 years with interest continuing at the current H bond interest rate).
Yield (Maximum—1975)	6% compounded semiannually if held to maturity. This interest is graduated starting at 4.99% the first year and increasing every 6 months for 10 years. Interest is exempt from state and local income taxes and is paid by Treasury checks semiannually beginning 6 months from the date on the bond. Bonds cashed before a 6-month interval lose interest.

	Bonds purchased during the month are dated and pay interest from the first day of the month.
Call Provision	Not callable.
Anticipated Profit or Loss (other than interest income)	No anticipated profit or loss because they can never be sold to other investors.
Safety	The repayment of their purchase price as well as the payment of interest is guaranteed by the U.S. government.
How Much Liquidity?	Bonds can be cashed for their original cost any time after the first 6 months except the month preceeding an interest payment. They cannot be borrowed against.

U.S. RETIREMENT BONDS

You have probably heard a lot about the Individual Retirement Account (IRA) and the Keogh Plan, and now you will be aware of how they can save you tax dollars. If you are self-employed or an employee not covered by a pension or profit-sharing plan, you can save yourself hundreds or even thousands of dollars every year in income taxes by taking advantage of retirement plans allowed by the U.S. government.

The IRA and the Keogh Plan allow you to contribute part of your earned income every year to your own tax-sheltered retirement plan. You are allowed to deduct the amount you contribute on your federal tax return, and sometimes your state tax return. The payment of income tax is postponed until years later, when you withdraw this money from your retirement plan. This income tax postponement is a very valuable tax benefit because you contribute money to your retirement plan in your working years, when you are in a high tax bracket, but you pay income tax when you withdraw your money from your retirement plan, when you most likely will be retired and in a lower tax bracket. Retirement plans offer double benefits to working couples because they can deduct retirement funds for two people.

If you are an employee not covered by a pension or profit-sharing plan, under the IRA you can postpone paying taxes on up to $1,500 or 15% of your gross annual income (whichever is less); and if you are self-employed, under the Keogh Plan you can postpone paying taxes on up to $7,500 or 15% of your gross annual income (whichever is less). Furthermore, both retirement plans allow you to postpone paying taxes on the interest, the dividends and the capital gains your retirement funds earn. Then, when you are 59½ years old or older, you are allowed to withdraw this money as often as you choose. There are two exceptions to this: If you are permanently disabled, your retirement funds can be withdrawn immediately; and in the event of death, your beneficiary is allowed to withdraw these funds at any time (up to five years). These retirement plans give added security to your future, give increased protection to your loved ones, in the event of death, and at the same time, give you a valuable income tax benefit.

The money you contribute to your retirement plan must be invested in a trust account, in a retirement savings account in any type of bank, in an annuity contract sold by an insurance company or in U.S. government retirement bonds. Banks advertise retirement savings accounts, insurance salespeople tell you about annuity contracts; however, you rarely hear about U.S. retirement bonds, which can be purchased for $50, $100 or $500. Since U.S. retirement bonds are guaranteed by the U.S. government, they have unequaled safety. This eliminates any worry as to whether a bank or an insurance company will still be in business when you retire.

In 1975, U.S. retirement bonds paid 6% annual interest compounded semiannually, which was a lower rate than other retirement plans pay, but retirement bond interest is not reduced by commission charges, annual fees, management fees or redemption charges. In addition, this interest is worth even more because it is exempt from state and local income taxes. After taking these factors into consideration, you may find that U.S. retirement bonds pay a higher net yield than other retirement plans.

Retirement bonds can be purchased and redeemed by mail or in person. All you do is call or write your Federal Reserve Bank and request application form PD

4345 if you are an employee and form PD 3550 if you
are self-employed. Then mail back or return in person
the completed application with your personal check or
a bank check for the amount of bonds you want to
purchase.

You can purchase retirement bonds as frequently or
infrequently as your circumstances permit. As long as
you send the application and check for retirement
bonds in plenty of time for the bonds to be dated in
December, they can be deducted from your income tax
return that year. Then, at 59½ years old, you can redeem them as frequently or infrequently as you choose.

The following charts give detailed information on
U.S. individual retirement bonds which qualify for the
IRA and are for employees not covered by a pension or
profit-sharing plan, and also on U.S. retirement plan
bonds which qualify for the Keogh Plan and are for the
self-employed.

U.S. INDIVIDUAL RETIREMENT BONDS
(Qualify for Individual Retirement Account)

Type of Security

IOUs of the U.S. government
—registered certificates. They
are for employees not
covered by other retirement
plans. Every year, employees
can purchase bonds worth
15% of their gross earned
annual income or $1,500
(whichever is less) and then
deduct these amounts from
their federal income tax.

Purchase Prices

$50, $100, $500.

Where to Buy and
Redeem

At Federal Reserve Banks by
mail or in person (request
form PD 4345). There are no
purchase or redemption
charges and no management
fees.

Maturity Date

When the owner reaches
70½ years old or 5 years
after the owner's death
(whichever is sooner).
However, they can be cashed
when the owner reaches 59½
years old without penalty.

Yield (Maximum—
1975)

6% compounded semi-
annually and paid when
cashed. Interest is exempt
from state and local income
taxes, and federal income tax

is postponed on the purchase price as well as on the interest until they are cashed. Bonds purchased at the end of the month are dated and pay interest from the first day of the month.

Call Provision	Not callable.
Anticipated Profit or Loss (other than interest income)	No anticipated profit or loss because they cannot be sold to other investors.
Safety	The repayment of their purchase price as well as the payment of interest is guaranteed by the U.S. government.
How Much Liquidity?	The U.S. government will cash bonds without penalty before maturity if the owner is permanently disabled, when the owner reaches 59½ years old or to transfer cash to other retirement plans. Bonds can be cashed within the first 12 months without interest. After that, they can be cashed at any time but are subject to a 10% tax penalty on the total amount (interest as well as principal). They cannot be borrowed against.

U.S. RETIREMENT PLAN BONDS
(Qualify for the Keogh Plan)

Type of Security

IOUs of the U.S. government —registered certificates. They are for self-employed individuals (also they qualify for pension and profit-sharing plans). The IRS must approve a retirement plan, and every year the self-employed can purchase bonds worth 15% of their gross earned annual income or $7,500 (whichever is less) and then deduct these amounts from their federal income tax.

Purchase Prices

$50, $100, $500, $1,000.

Where to Buy and Redeem

At Federal Reserve Banks by mail or in person (request form PD 3550). There are no purchase or redemption charges and no management fees.

Maturity Date

Not before owner reaches 59½ years old and not longer than 5 years after owner's death.

Yield (Maximum— 1975)

6% compounded semi-annually and paid when cashed. Interest is exempt from state and local income taxes. Federal income tax is postponed on the purchase price as well as on the interest until they are cashed. Bonds purchased during the month are dated and pay interest from the first day of the month.

*C*all Provision	Not callable.
*A*nticipated Profit or Loss (other than interest income)	No anticipated profit or loss because they cannot be sold to other investors.
*S*afety	The repayment of their purchase prices as well as the payment of interest is guaranteed by the U.S. government.
*H*ow Much Liquidity?	The U.S. government will not cash bonds for an owner before maturity unless the owner becomes permanently disabled. The beneficiary can cash bonds in the event of the owner's death. They cannot be borrowed against.

TREASURY SECURITIES

Treasury securities are another type of U.S. government time deposits, a type which you are probably not familiar with. As a result, the next twenty pages are the most difficult in this book. Plan to read them slowly. They may even require several readings.

Treasury securities usually pay a higher rate of interest than U.S. savings bonds, U.S. retirement bonds or bank savings accounts. Treasury securities allow you to deposit $1,000 or more directly with the U.S. government for three months to thirty years. The government pays you interest and repays the face value of Treasury securities when they come due. Furthermore, you can borrow against Treasury securities (use them as collateral for a loan).

Treasury time deposits differ from bank time deposits in that you can deposit money in bank time deposits at any time, but you can deposit money in new Treasury securities only on the few days a month the U.S. government sells them. Also, the bank normally cashes time deposits before they come due, whereas the U.S. government cashes Treasury securities only on the date they come due. Despite this, you can buy Treasury securities or get cash for them at any time. Why? Because you can buy secondhand Treasury securities any time from other investors and you can also get cash any time by selling Treasury securities to other investors. Secondhand Treasury securities trade in the Government Securities Market with their remaining maturities (days, months or years) in billion-dollar volume every trading day—the same way stocks trade.

The market price you receive if you sell Treasury securities before maturity may be more or less than the price you paid. Why? Because the market prices of

Treasury securities constantly go up and down with changes in interest rates. In other words, if you sell secondhand Treasury securities that pay a higher fixed rate of interest than new ones, other investors will pay you a higher market price, and if you sell secondhand Treasury securities that pay a lower fixed rate of interest than new ones other investors will pay you a lower market price (more about this later, see page 77).

The marketability of Treasury securities adds a new and exciting dimension to time deposit investing. You have the opportunity to trade Treasury securities during their lifetime like stocks, and yet you also have the security of receiving repayment of their face value at maturity like bank time deposits. By selecting a maturity date (see page 15) that allows you to leave your cash deposited in Treasury securities until they come due, you eliminate the risk of loss. That way, should the market price of your Treasury securities rise, you can sell them before maturity for a profit, and should the market price of your Treasury securities decline, instead of taking a loss, you can hold them to maturity, when the U.S. government will repay their full face value.

Treasury securities are not limited to paying maximum interest rates set by federal law as are bank time deposits. Instead, interest rates on Treasury securities are determined in the open market by supply and demand (for more details, see page 66). That is why, in 1974, Treasury securities paid up to 4% more annual interest than government-regulated bank time deposits. In addition, interest on Treasury securities is worth even more because it is exempt from state and local income taxes. If you check bank annual reports, you will see that banks buy U.S. government securities. They reinvest some of your savings deposits in Treasury securities and usually make a profit.

You can buy new Treasury securities from Federal

Reserve Banks without paying a purchase charge, or you can buy new Treasury securities through the investment department of large commercial banks and brokerage firms, which usually charge a purchase fee of about $25 if you buy less than $100,000 worth. Federal Reserve Banks are the banks for the U.S. government, not for individuals, and they perform many banking services for the government—one such service is selling Treasury securities. The United States is divided into twelve Federal Reserve districts and each district has one Federal Reserve Bank (as well as a few branches). Your local commercial bank will give you the address of the nearest Federal Reserve Bank (or branch).

When you loan money to the government by purchasing government securities (government time deposits), you receive the government's bond, a general term for its promise to repay you on maturity date. Thus, bonds are often referred to by different names. These names identify their original maturity dates as well as their minimum prices. Treasury securities which are $10,000 time deposits with original maturities of three months to one year are called *Treasury bills;* Treasury securities which are $1,000 time deposits with original maturities of one to seven years are called *Treasury notes;* and Treasury securities which are $1,000 time deposits with original maturities of seven years or longer are called *Treasury bonds.*

Treasury Bills (T-bills)
New Treasury bills are three-, six- or twelve-month Treasury time deposits. You can remember Uncle Sam's Treasury *bills* come due in a short time, the same way that your day-to-day *bills* come due in a short time.

T-bills have minimum face values of $10,000; however, they always sell at a discount or for less than their face value. Why? Because T-bills pay interest by selling

for less than their face value just like Series E savings
bonds. Interest is the difference between the price you
pay for a T-bill and the face value you receive from the
government at maturity. For example, if you pay
$9,400 for a T-bill, the government will pay you
$10,000 (its face value) at maturity and your interest is
$600. But should you sell T-bills before maturity, your
interest is the difference between the price you pay and
the price you receive when you sell. For example, if you
pay $9,400 for a T-bill and sell it before maturity for
$9,600, your interest is $200.

The receipts or certificates the government gives you
when you buy T-bills are not registered in your name
as are your bankbooks and your savings bond certificates. As a result, they must be safeguarded like cash,
because whoever "bears" T-bill certificates can cash
them (that is why they are called bearer certificates).
So, T-*b*ills have *b*earer certificates and pay interest by
selling *b*elow their face value. The U.S. government
sells new T-bills every week and occasionally sells Tax
Anticipation bills (a type of T-bill) which can be profitably used to pay federal income taxes (for a detailed
account, see page 86).

When should you buy T-bills? If you want your
money repaid in one year or less, if the T-bills yield
more than other safe investments (as in 1974, when
their yields were as high as 10%) or if the future trend
of interest rates appears to be rising rapidly. In these
cases, their very short maturity dates can be an advantage because you will have the opportunity of reinvesting your savings at a higher rate of interest in a very
short time. Otherwise, the frequent buying of T-bills
maturing in one year or less can be troublesome for
you.

Treasury Notes

New Treasury notes are one- to ten-year Treasury time deposits that usually cost a minimum of $1,000, although sometimes the U.S. government raises this minimum price to $5,000 or $10,000). New Treasury notes sell for their face value and pay a fixed rate of interest twice a year just like Series H savings bonds. In other words, new Treasury notes usually sell for their $1,000 face value, and if they pay an 8% fixed rate of interest annually ($80 a year), you would receive $40 interest every six months until maturity, when the U.S. government repays their $1,000 face value.

Treasury notes offer you the choice of bearer or registered certificates. Bearer certificates do not have your name written on them, and your name is not registered with the U.S. government. They pay interest by coupons attached to their bearer certificates. Therefore, they are also called coupon certificates. Every six months on interest-payment date, you detach one coupon and cash it at your bank. Since bearer Treasury notes are presumed to belong to whomever has possession, they must be safeguarded like cash.

Registered Treasury notes, on the other hand, have your name written on the certificates as well as registered with the U.S. government. If they are lost or stolen, the government will replace them. Registered notes pay interest by Treasury checks mailed to you every six months until maturity. Although they are, of course, safer than bearer notes, there is one inconvenience: If you want to sell registered notes before maturity, they must be exchanged for bearer notes (coupon notes) at a Federal Reserve Bank, which can take many weeks. Occasionally, registered notes can be sold, but they sell for lower prices than coupon notes.

Treasury notes are excellent investments for both small and large investors. You can buy them for as little as $1,000 in safe, registered form and receive cash or Treasury checks for your interest every six months. In addition, if you select the shorter maturity dates of one to four years, Treasury notes offer some inflation protection. Why? Because you can usually reinvest your savings at a higher rate of interest every time they come due, which is a relatively short time. In 1974, Treasury notes paid up to 9% annual interest, interest that is worth even more because it is exempt from state and local income taxes.

Treasury Bonds

New Treasury bonds are ten- to thirty-year Treasury time deposits. Treasury bonds have minimum face values of $1,000. They sell for their face value and pay a fixed rate of interest twice a year just like Treasury notes. They also offer you the choice of coupon or registered certificates.

Some Treasury bonds have call provisions which shorten their maturities. A call provision allows the U.S. government to pay off the owners of Treasury bonds before they come due (usually five years before they mature for their face value). This is to your disadvantage because Uncle Sam only calls bonds if interest rates decline. Then he can replace bonds paying higher fixed rates of interest with bonds paying lower fixed rates of interest. Be sure to check for a call provision when buying Treasury bonds, particularly if the bonds you are considering pay a high fixed rate of interest, since these are the bonds most likely to be called.

There are certain issues of secondhand Treasury bonds called Flower bonds. Flower bonds can be profitably used to pay federal estate taxes (for more details, see the discussion of Flower bonds on page 91).

Treasury bonds are good investments whenever the economy heads into a deep recession or a depression (deflationary times). During those periods interest rates usually decline, so you want to lock in the current higher interest rates for a long time. In 1974, Treasury bonds paid up to 8.6% annual interest, interest that is exempt from state and local income taxes, which makes it worth even more.

How to Buy New Treasury Securities from Federal Reserve Banks

Anyone with $1,000 or more can buy new Treasury securities from Federal Reserve Banks on the days they are sold and pay no purchase charge. Large investors buying a minimum of $200,000 worth are usually required to compete for the Treasury securities the government is selling. They must submit competitive bids stating the specific rate of interest they want the government to pay them. Sometimes they buy Treasury securities and sometimes they do not. Naturally, the government wants to pay the lowest possible interest rates, so whenever the competitive bids outnumber the Treasury securities for sale, the U.S. government accepts only the competitive bids with the lowest interest rates. However, should the Treasury securities for sale outnumber the bids submitted, the government generally accepts all bids, those with lower interest rates as well as those with higher interest rates.

If you want to buy less than $200,000 worth, you automatically buy new Treasury securities by submitting a noncompetitive bid (a letter) and your money. You do not state a specific rate of interest you want the government to pay you because you generally receive the average of all the rates of interest paid to the large competitive bidders at that auction.

The government sells (auctions) Treasury bills every week, but it does not auction notes and bonds on a regular schedule. You can request advance notices of all Treasury auctions (or of only Treasury note and Treasury bond auctions) by calling or writing the nearest

Federal Reserve Bank (any commercial bank will give you the telephone number and address). It normally takes about five weeks for the first advance notice to arrive. After that, notices arrive two to three days before every Treasury auction, which gives you just enough time to buy Treasury securities before the last accepted postmark date for that auction.

The information in advance notices is mostly for the large investors who submit competitive bids. If you are buying less than $200,000 worth, you can disregard most of this information because you need to locate only five items in this notice. Then you can write a short letter which serves as your noncompetitive bid.

Let's assume you receive an advance notice for the sale of Treasury notes and you want to buy two $1,000 Treasury notes. You find the following information in the advance notice: (1) type of security being sold (in this case, Treasury notes); (2) the minimum price (in this case, $1,000); (3) the series (in this case, E-1977); (4) the date the securities come due (in this case, November 1, 1977); (5) last accepted postmark date for noncompetitive bids at this auction (in this case, October 26, 1975). Use this information to write the following letter to be submitted as your noncompetitive tender (bid), and enclose a bank cashier check or certified check for the face value of the Treasury notes you want to buy (in this case, $2,000).

October 24, 1975

To Whom It May Concern:

This is my noncompetitive tender for two registered ($1,000) Treasury notes of the new series (E-1977) maturing (November 1, 1977). Please mail my Treasury notes in registered form made out to (name with the social security number and possibly a second name as co-owner). A check for ($2,000) is enclosed made payable to the Federal Reserve Bank. Kindly send the registered Treasury notes to the address below. Thank you.

Sincerely,

Street Address
City, State and Zip Code

Mail your letter and check to the nearest Federal Reserve Bank or branch no later than the last accepted postmark date for noncompetitive bids (in this case, October 26, 1975). On the outside of the envelope write in large letters TENDER FOR TREASURY NOTES. You can also use this same letter to buy Treasury bills or Treasury bonds by merely changing a few words.

Since interest rates paid by new Treasury securities are usually not established until after you submit your money, sometimes you are charged a small additional amount or refunded a small amount when you buy new Treasury notes or bonds. Why? Because Treasury notes and bonds pay a fixed rate of interest to the nearest $\frac{1}{8}$ of 1%, whereas the Treasury accepts competitive bids for their interest rates to the nearest $1/100$ of 1%, and this can cause a difference of a few cents for each $1,000 you submit.

If you buy $10,000 worth of Treasury bills (or any amount up to $200,000) from Federal Reserve Banks, you submit a check for their $10,000 face value. Then immediately following the auction, you will receive a Treasury check for the difference between the $10,000 face value you submitted and the average discount price that was established by the accepted competitive bids at that auction.

Federal Reserve Banks deliver new Treasury securities to you by mail or in person, but they will not hold securities in safekeeping for individuals. Since taking physical possession of bearer Treasury securities (which are the equivalent of cash) is risky, it is safer to buy only registered Treasury notes and bonds at Federal Reserve Banks.

It usually takes six to eight weeks for Federal Reserve Banks to register Treasury securities. Whenever you receive your Treasury securities (whether bearer or registered form) keep them in a safe place, preferably a safety deposit box. In addition, make a separate record of the serial numbers, the dates of issue, the maturity dates, the fixed rates of interest and the interest-payment dates. Although registered notes can be replaced if they are lost or stolen, this takes time and effort.

You can redeem Treasury securities for cash (by mail or in person) when they come due at Federal Reserve Banks (or branches) without paying a charge. You can also exchange maturing securities for new securities being sold at that time; this is called rolling them over. For more details, contact the nearest Federal Reserve Bank.

How to Buy New Treasury Securities from Banks and Brokerage Firms
Large commercial banks and large brokerage firms will buy new Treasury securities for you through Federal Reserve Banks. They will hold your securities for safekeeping and they will credit your account with interest on interest-payment dates. Furthermore, when your Treasury securities come due, they will redeem them for you and credit your account. For these services, they generally charge a service fee of about $25. Fees vary and should be checked, but if you purchase amounts of $100,000 or more, there is usually no charge.

Banks that are members of the Federal Reserve System can hold your Treasury securities for safekeeping in Federal Reserve Bank vaults, the safest place. Federal Reserve Banks merely credit Treasury securities to the account of their member banks by bookkeeping entries. Your bank then gives you a receipt stating your securities are being held for safekeeping in a Federal Reserve Bank vault.

Buying Treasury securities through banks and brokerage firms is much less work than buying them directly from Federal Reserve Banks. But if you pay a service charge, your net yield is less than had you bought them directly from the latter.

When you buy or sell Treasury securities at banks or brokerage firms, you are leaving cash or securities in your account for varying periods of time. That is why it is important to select financially sound banks and brokerage firms to do business with. You already know the guidelines for selecting a bank with a solid foundation (see page 8), but how do you determine which brokerage firms are more likely to have solid foundations?

Large brokerage firms that are members of the New York Stock Exchange, members of the Securities Investment Protection Corporation (SIPC) and whose liabilities are less than ten times their net capital are more likely to be financially sound. Here's why. Brokerage firms with capital of $10 million or more have a large financial base, which generally gives them more strength. Firms that are members of the New York Stock Exchange are examined regularly and are subject to surprise audits, and if they are members of the SIPC you get double protection. The SIPC, a self-supporting corporation with limited borrowing privileges from the U.S. government, protects brokerage firm accounts much like the FDIC or FSLIC protects bank accounts. If the brokerage firm fails, the SIPC promises to repay a total of $50,000 for securities or cash left by investors in their brokerage firm accounts. Of this $50,000 total, a maximum of $20,000 is paid for the cash in an account. (This, of course, does not insure you against market losses.) In 1975, the SIPC asked Congress to double these amounts, so check for the amount of protection the SIPC gives your account currently. Most large brokerage firms not only give your account protection with the SIPC but also insure your account for an even larger amount with reputable insurance companies.

Brokerage firms whose liabilities are less than ten times their net capital are less likely to have financial problems. You can check this ratio easily by calling any brokerage firm and requesting its recent balance sheet (published every six months). This ratio is called the net capital requirement and is listed in a footnote on the balance sheet or in a separate section called Notes to Balance Sheet.

How do you locate brokerage firms more likely to have solid foundations? You write the New York Stock Exchange, 11 Wall Street, New York, N.Y., 10005, to the attention of the Investor Service Bureau, and request the names of the member firms in your area. Then you can call the brokerage firms you are considering and find out if they are members of the SIPC. You can also request their current balance sheets in order to check to see if their total capital is $10 million or more and if their liabilities are less than ten times their capital.

In case you want to deal with a brokerage firm that does not meet all these requirements, you can do business on a cash basis by making prior arrangements with your bank. When you buy securities, you can ask the broker to deliver them to your bank. The bank will pay for the securities by charging your bank account and will keep them in the bank vault until you pick them up. When you sell securities, you can deliver them to your bank rather than to your brokerage firm. On settlement date, the broker picks them up at the bank and pays for them with a cashier check in the amount of the total sale price, which is credited to your bank account. That way, you never leave cash or securities at the brokerage firm. Before you trade on a cash basis, you should check the bank's charge for this service. If you are a good customer of the bank, sometimes there is no charge, and at other times there is a nominal fee for this service.

Why You Use the Word *Yield*

Since the word *yield* is troublesome, why not use the word *interest* instead? Because while sometimes the yield from an investment is the same as the interest it pays, most times, the yield is either more or less than the interest. For example, the yield from government securities is more than the interest they pay. Since you are not required to pay state or local income taxes on interest from government securities, you keep more of this interest, which increases your yield. On the other hand, if you pay a $25 purchase charge to buy Treasury securities, your yield is less than the interest Treasury securities pay—it is reduced by the $25 purchase charge. Therefore, the word *yield* is used because it expresses the total income you actually keep after you make all the necessary adjustments.

How to Use Treasury Securities to Your Advantage

It is convenient to deposit money in passbook savings accounts because you can normally withdraw it at any time without a penalty. It is comfortable to deposit money in savings bonds guaranteed by the U.S. government because you are allowed to withdraw cash without penalty after the first few months. However, it is usually more profitable to invest money over the amount you need for day-to-day living expenses and emergencies in Treasury securities, for these are directly guaranteed by the U.S. government and, if held

to maturity, generally yield more than savings accounts
or savings bonds.

Let's briefly review the MY CASH checklist for Treasury securities. This information will help you compare
Treasury securities with other investments in order to
determine the better buy.

Treasury securities offer *M*aturity dates from days to
thirty years. Their *Y*ields are worth more because their
interest is exempt from state and local income taxes.
Only Treasury bonds have *C*all provisions, which
should be checked before you buy bonds. You can
*A*nticipate a profit if you sell Treasury notes or bonds
yielding more than new ones and a loss if you sell Treasury notes or bonds yielding less than new ones. Treasury securities held to maturity offer maximum *S*afety
because they are directly guaranteed by the U.S. government.

*H*ow much liquidity do Treasury securities offer?
They are sold in larger volume than all other securities,
so there are more ready buyers to give you cash for
them than for any other security. In addition, you can
borrow against Treasury securities at your bank and
usually pay about 1% more than the prime rate of interest which may be a higher or lower rate of interest than
your Treasury securities pay. In other words, if you own
Treasury securities paying an 8¾% rate of interest and
need the money for them before maturity, when the
prime rate is 6½% it is more profitable to borrow
against them than it is to sell them. Why? Because you
can continue to collect the 8¾% interest they pay
(even though the bank holds them as collateral for your
loan) and you pay the bank only about 7½% interest on
the money you borrow. If the prime rate is 8%, you
must pay the bank about 9% interest, and then borrowing against Treasury securities is not profitable. By contrast, if you borrow against bank time deposits, federal
law requires that you must pay the bank at least 1%
more interest than bank time deposits pay you.

Shirley Wrong Attempts to Buy New Treasury Securities

Shirley Wrong requests advance notices for all Treasury auctions from the nearest Federal Reserve Bank. After waiting for several weeks, she finally receives a notice for the auction of four-year Treasury notes which she does not understand. She takes the notice to a bank officer who suggests it is more convenient to deposit her money in a four-year bank time deposit. Then, instead of contacting a Federal Reserve Bank to find out how to buy the Treasury notes being auctioned —which offer unequaled safety, tax benefits and at that time paid 8¾% annual interest—she deposits her money in a bank time deposit paying 7¼% interest— *she is surely wrong.*

Shirley Wright Buys New Treasury Notes

Shirley Wright calls the nearest Federal Reserve Bank and requests advance notices of Treasury auctions. Several weeks later, the notices begin to arrive. Most of the time, she glances at them and throws them away. However, several months later, when she has $10,000 to invest, she takes the time to read these notices more carefully.

In order to decide which Treasury securities to buy, she first has to determine what maturity date fits her needs. Since she has a steady monthly salary as well as $1,500 in a bank account and $1,000 deposited in Series H savings bonds, she will not, under normal circumstances, need this $10,000 for day-to-day living expenses or emergencies. She therefore looks to the trend of future interest rates to select a maturity date. She notices that the demand for business loans announced weekly by the Federal Reserve Bank of New York is declining and that the prime rate of interest is slowly being lowered. Although inflation seems to be built into the U.S. economy for the long haul, she believes there may be a deflationary period for several years causing interest rates to decline temporarily. Therefore, she selects a two- to four-year maturity date in order to lock in the current high interest rate for two to four years.

Most of the advance notices she receives are for auctions of T-bills with maturities of one year or less, but eventually she receives a notice for the auction of four-year Treasury notes. She calls the investment department of her commercial bank and finds out that second-hand Treasury securities coming due in about four years are currently yielding 8¾%. Next she approximates the Treasury notes being auctioned in a couple of days will also pay about 8¾% annual interest. Then she uses the MY CASH checklist to compare four-year Treasury notes with four-year bank time deposits to determine the better buy. Treasury notes are a little safer, can be sold to other investors for a profit if their market prices rise, offer more liquidity and yield even more than the four-year bank time deposit.

It is now obvious to Shirley that the four-year Treasury notes being auctioned are the better buy. She uses the sample letter for buying Treasury securities (see page 68), substituting the current information she locates in the advance notice. She buys a $10,000 bank cashier check made payable to the Federal Reserve Bank and mails her letter and check to the nearest Federal Reserve Bank before the last postmark date required for noncompetitive bids (tenders) at that auction. She writes on the outside of the envelope in large letters TENDER FOR TREASURY NOTES.

The day after the auction, Shirley reads on the financial page of the newspaper that the four-year Treasury notes auctioned paid the average annual interest rate of 8¾% (the amount of interest she will receive for four years). Weeks later, her ten $1,000 registered notes arrive by mail. She makes a separate record of serial numbers, maturity dates, fixed rates of interest, face value and interest-payment dates. The next time Shirley goes to the bank, she puts her registered notes in her safety deposit box. She may sell them before maturity if she can make a profit. Otherwise, a few weeks before maturity, she plans to mail them back to the Federal Reserve Bank and exchange them for new Treasury securities. She feels very comfortable with her $10,000 investment in four-year Treasury time deposits—*she is surely right.*

How Secondhand Treasury Securities Trade
Although you usually plan to keep Treasury securities to maturity, there may be times when you want to sell them before this date. Furthermore, at some time, you may want to buy secondhand Treasury securities rather than new ones. For this reason we are going to discuss how secondhand securities are bought and sold in the Government Securities Market.

The market prices for Treasury securities are the prices investors will pay for their face values. These market prices change every time interest rates change. In other words, the market price you receive if you sell Treasury securities before maturity depends on what has happened to interest rates since the securities were originally sold by the U.S. government. Why? Because in order to have a market where secondhand Treasury securities can trade, they must yield the same as new ones. Otherwise, investors would not buy secondhand Treasury securities yielding 7% if new ones were yielding 8%, and investors would not sell secondhand Treasury securities yielding 9% if new ones were yielding 8%.

Since interest is paid differently by T-bills than it is by Treasury notes and bonds, there must be two different ways that secondhand Treasury securities adjust to yield the same as new ones. We will discuss each of the two ways separately—how secondhand T-bills adjust and then how secondhand Treasury notes and bonds adjust.

How Secondhand T-bills Yield the Same As New Ones

T-bills pay interest by selling for less than their $10,000 face value. This allows T-bills to pay any amount of interest by selling for varying prices less than their face value (discount prices). In other words, T-bills pay $500 interest by selling for $500 less than their $10,000 face value, that is, for the discount price of $9,500; or T-bills pay $100 interest by selling for $100 less than their $10,000 face value, that is, for the discount price of $9,900. Because T-bill interest is flexible, whenever interest rates change, the market prices (the discount prices that T-bills sell for) of secondhand T-bills change to the same discount price that new T-bills sell for. That way, secondhand T-bills pay the same amount of interest and yield the same as new ones. For example, when new T-bills (maturing in three months) pay $200 interest, they sell for the discount price of $9,800. Thus, the market prices for secondhand T-bills (maturing in three months) would also be the same discount price of $9,800.

How Secondhand Treasury Notes and Bonds Yield the Same As New Ones

Treasury notes and Treasury bonds pay their original fixed rate of interest every year until they come due. For example, $1,000 notes and bonds with an 8% fixed rate of interest pay $40 every six months for a total of $80 interest a year. This interest is paid separately by Treasury checks or coupons. It is called a fixed rate of interest because it is fixed when new notes and bonds are originally sold and never changes until they mature (or are called).

How, then, can secondhand Treasury notes and bonds yield the same as new ones? Since new notes and bonds sell for their $1,000 face value, secondhand ones can adjust to yield the same by selling for market prices that are more or less than their $1,000 face value. For example, you would pay a premium of about $34 more than face value, or a market price of $1,034, for second-hand four-year Treasury notes that pay 9% fixed interest when new notes pay only 8%. At maturity, you would lose the $34 premium over face value you paid because the U.S. government repays only the $1,000 face value. But after you subtract the $34 premium from the higher 9% fixed interest you receive for four years, these secondhand notes yield the same as new ones—8%.

On the other hand, if you buy secondhand four-year notes that pay a 7% fixed rate of interest when new ones pay 8%, you would pay about $34 less than their face value, or a market price of $966. At maturity, you would receive $34 more than the $966 discount market price you paid because the U.S. government repays the $1,000 face value. But after you add the $34 discount income to the lower 7% fixed interest you receive for four years, these secondhand notes yield the same as new ones—8%. Discount income is attractive because if you own Treasury notes or bonds for six months or longer, the Internal Revenue Code states this income can normally be taxed at one-half the ordinary tax rate (capital gains rate), whereas regular interest income is taxed at the ordinary income tax rate.

The yield of secondhand Treasury notes and bonds that is reduced at maturity because they sell for a premium or that is increased at maturity because they sell for a discount is called the yield to maturity. Since discount income offers a tax advantage, secondhand Treasury notes and bonds selling for a discount generally pay a lower yield to maturity than secondhand Treasury notes and bonds selling for a premium.

When you sell secondhand Treasury notes and bonds, you receive the market price plus the interest they have earned since the last interest-payment date (accrued interest). Although Treasury notes and bonds only pay interest at six-month intervals, their interest accumulates (accrues) every day, and that is why the buyer pays you accrued interest. Of course, if you buy secondhand Treasury notes and bonds, you pay the seller accrued interest.

Buying and Selling Secondhand Treasury Securities
Secondhand Treasury securities are not sold at Federal Reserve Banks. You can only buy (or sell) them from the investment department of large commercial banks or brokerage firms. You are generally charged a $25 service fee; however, fees vary and should be checked before an order is placed. Furthermore, if you buy a minimum of $100,000 of Treasury securities, there is usually no charge. You can shop around for secondhand Treasury securities because when banks or brokerage firms hold the ones you want to buy in inventory, they often give you a better price.

The Advantages of Buying and Selling Secondhand Securities
New Treasury securities can be bought from Federal Reserve Banks without paying a service charge. Furthermore, when you buy them from Federal Reserve Banks, you receive the average rate of interest paid to the largest investors at that time, and this is generally a higher rate than you would receive if you bought less than $100,000 worth of secondhand Treasury securities (less than $100,000 is considered an odd lot and therefore pays a lower yield).

Why, then, would you ever buy secondhand Treasury securities? Because you can buy secondhand securities every day, whereas you can buy new securities only on the few days a month the U.S. government sells them. Also, you can buy secondhand securities with remaining maturities of a few days to almost thirty years, whereas new securities offer only one specific maturity date. In addition, you can buy secondhand notes and bonds at face value (which pay income at their fixed rate of interest), above face value (which pay income at their fixed rate of interest reduced by a premium) or below face value (which pay income at their fixed rate of interest increased by discount income). Secondhand Treasury notes and bonds pay income in three ways and you can select the way that is to your tax benefit. On the other hand, new notes and bonds sell for their face value (and pay income only one way at their fixed rate of interest).

What happens if you decide to sell Treasury securities before maturity? You always receive interest for every day you have owned them, and the closer they are to maturity, the more likely you are to receive a market price close to their face value. For example, if you need cash for six-year $10,000 Treasury notes paying 7¾% interest at the end of five years, you would receive their interest for every day you held them, or $3,875. When you add the interest to what past records indicate their market price could be—between $9,600 and $11,400—you would receive a total of $13,475 to $15,275. By contrast, if you need cash for a six-year $10,000 bank time deposit paying 7¾% interest at the end of five years, you would receive your original $10,000 savings deposit plus only $2493.75 interest for a total of $12,493.75, which is much less than $10,000 Treasury notes paying the same rate of interest would bring. Why? Because the longer you hold bank deposits to maturity, the larger the interest penalty you pay if you need cash before maturity—there is a three months' loss of interest, and the interest you earned for all five years reverts to the lower passbook savings interest rate—whereas the longer you hold Treasury notes to maturity, the smaller the penalty if you need cash before maturity.

Shirley Wright Sells Her Treasury Notes
Shirley has been following the market price of her
$10,000 Treasury notes in the financial section of her
local newspaper listed under Treasury bonds.

Yield Chart to go here

She identifies her notes by their fixed rate of interest
—8¾s; by their maturity date—August, 1978n; and by
the little n after the maturity date which signifies they
are notes rather than bonds. The bid price (103.28) is
the amount she receives if she sells these notes and the
asked price (104.4) is the price she has to pay if she
wants to buy these notes. The difference between the
bid and asked prices is the commission the bank or
brokerage firm makes. The bid change is +8, which
means these notes sell for 8/32 more than they did on
the previous trading day. The 7.08 yield is the yield to
maturity (8¾% fixed rate of interest reduced by the
premium they sell for over their $1,000 face value).

Since the bid price of 103.28 is for million-dollar
trades, Shirley approximates that she will receive
$1,030 for each of her ten notes ($10,300 total). Treasury securities are quoted as 100 for each $1,000, so she
adds a 0 to the dollar price of 103 to approximate
$1,030 per note (she disregards the numbers after the
decimal point, .28, which is 28/32). She decides to sell
them and take a $300 profit.

Although sometimes Treasury notes can be sold in
registered form, they always bring lower market prices.
Therefore, Shirley decides to exchange her registered
notes for coupon notes before she sells them (had she
originally bought coupon notes she would have sold
them immediately). She calls the nearest Federal Reserve Bank for instructions to exchange registered

notes for coupon notes, which she then follows. She takes her registered notes from her safety deposit box and has a bank officer guarantee her signature with an issuing agent stamp (not a notary public endorsement). She also asks the bank officer for form PD 3905, which she fills in. Under mailing instructions, she lists the address of the investment department of her bank. That way, she never has to take physical possession of coupon Treasury notes, which are the same as cash. She sends the completed form with her registered notes to the nearest Federal Reserve Bank (by registered insured mail). She also alerts the head of the investment department at her bank that her $10,000 coupon Treasury notes will be arriving from the Federal Reserve Bank and asks to be notified as soon as they are received.

Six weeks later, the investment department of the bank calls Shirley to tell her that her coupon Treasury notes have arrived. She finds out the bank charges $25 to sell them and the best price the bank offers for her ten Treasury notes is $10,305. She decides to sell them.

After deducting the $25 bank charge, Shirley receives the net price of $10,270 plus $347 accrued interest. The next day the bank credits her account with a total of $10,617. When she includes the interest the government has already paid her, she figures her $10,000 investment in Treasury notes has returned $11,054 in less than one year. She is happy with the way her savings are working for her—*she is surely right.*

P.S. Shirley plans to invest her $11,000 in new Treasury notes in the next few months when she anticipates interest rates will rise again. She also is going to continue reinvesting her interest and hopes to double her original $10,000 investment in eight or nine years. What a comfortable way to have her money grow.

The following outline accounts of Treasury bills, Tax Anticipation bills, Treasury notes, Treasury bonds and Flower bonds were helpful to Shirley Wright when she compared Treasury securities with other investments as well as when she bought Treasury securities.

TREASURY BILLS (T-Bills)

Type of Security	IOUs of the U.S. government —bearer certificates
Face or Par Values (Redemption Prices)	$10,000, $15,000, $50,000, $100,000, $1 million.*
Where to Buy, Sell and Redeem	New T-bills are bought at Federal Reserve Banks (no commission charge); new and secondhand T-bills are bought and sold at banks or brokerage firms (charge of about $25 and usually no charge for trades of $100,000 or more). They are redeemed at maturity wherever bought (no charge). These charges can vary and should be checked before an order is placed.
Maturity Dates (New T-bills)	3, 6 and 12 months (3- and 6-month maturities are auctioned every Monday; 12-month maturities are auctioned once a month on Tuesday).

Yield (Maximum—1975)	7.28% Interest is paid by selling for less than face value and is exempt from state and local income taxes.
Call Provision	Not callable.
Anticipated Profit or Loss (other than interest income)	There can be no anticipated profit or loss because the difference between their purchase price and redemption price (or sale price) is always interest. Furthermore, the Internal Revenue Code states that this income is taxed as ordinary interest income—not a profit or a loss.
Safety	The repayment of their face value, which includes interest, is guaranteed by the U.S. government.
How Much Liquidity?	The most easily sold of all securities, which is why they are considered almost the equivalent of cash. T-bills can be borrowed against at any bank for about 1% above the current prime rate.

*In 1975, the Treasury sold new Federal Fund bills for a minimum of $10 million that mature in approximately 2 weeks.

TAX ANTICIPATION BILLS (TABS)

TABs are T-bills and have all the same characteristics
as T-bills (see account of T-bills). TABs are not issued on
a regular schedule and can be issued for any length of
time less than one year, but they always mature a day
or so after quarterly income tax payments are due.
They are most profitable when used as payment of federal income tax, as the U.S. government will accept
them at face value in payment of income tax a day or
so before maturity. They are most frequently bought by
large corporations making large income tax payments.
Any Federal Reserve Bank will issue a receipt for Tax
Anticipation bills; this receipt is attached to the federal
income tax return in payment of federal income tax.

TABs usually pay a slightly lower yield because of
their income tax benefit. However, when they pay the
same yield as other Treasury bills, they can be purchased if their maturity date meets your needs.

TREASURY NOTES

Type of Security	IOUs of the U.S. government —coupon or registered certificates.
Face or Par Values (Redemption Prices)	$1,000, $5,000, $10,000, $100,000, $1 million.
Where to Buy, Sell and Redeem	New notes are bought at Federal Reserve Banks (no commission charge); new and secondhand notes are bought and sold at banks or brokerage firms (charge of about $25 and usually no charge for trades of $100,000 or more). They are redeemed at maturity wherever bought (no charge). These charges can vary and should be checked before an order is placed.
Maturity Date (New notes)	1 to 10 years.
Yield (Maximum—1975)	8.5%. Interest is paid semiannually and is exempt from state and local income taxes.
Call Provision	Not callable.

*A*nticipated Profit or Loss (other than interest income)	Anticipated profit if the notes sold before maturity yield more than new ones; anticipated loss if the notes sold yield less than new ones.
*S*afety	The repayment of their face value as well as interest is guaranteed by the U.S. government.
*H*ow Much Liquidity?	Notes trade actively and can be easily sold for cash every trading day or can be borrowed against at a bank for at least 1% above the current prime rate.

TREASURY BONDS

Type of Security	IOUs of the U.S. government —coupon or registered certificates.
Face or Par Values (Redemption Prices)	$1,000, $5,000, $10,000, $100,000, $1 million.
Where to Buy, Sell and Redeem	New bonds are bought at Federal Reserve Banks (no commission charge); new and secondhand bonds are bought and sold at banks or brokerage firms (charge of about $25 and usually no charge for trades of $100,000 or more). They are redeemed at maturity wherever bought (no charge). These charges can vary and should be checked before an order is placed.
Maturity Dates (New bonds)	10 years and over.
Yield (Maximum— 1975)	8.5% Interest is paid semiannually and is exempt from state and local income taxes.
Call Provision	Sometimes callable their last 5 years of maturity at face value.

Anticipated Profit or Loss (other than interest income)	Anticipated profit if the bonds sold before maturity yield more than new ones; anticipated loss if the bonds sold yield less than new ones.
Safety	The repayment of their face value and interest are guaranteed by the U.S. government.
How Much Liquidity?	Bonds can be sold for cash every trading day or can be borrowed against at a bank for at least 1% above the current prime rate.

TREASURY BONDS FOR ESTATE
PLANNING—FLOWER BONDS
(Old Only)

These are secondhand Treasury bonds and have all the same characteristics as Treasury bonds schedule (see preceding page). Flower bonds are specific issues of secondhand Treasury bonds that can be used for estate planning. They can be bought below face value and used at face value, before maturity, to pay federal estate tax (if they were owned by the deceased person at the time of death). Because of these estate tax benefits, Flower bonds yield much less than other secondhand Treasury bonds. They are supposedly called Flower bonds because the extra value allowed by the U.S. government pays for the flowers at the funeral. The following Treasury bonds are Flower bonds:

Fixed Rate		Call Year	Maturity Year
2¾%	April 1,	1975	1980
4¼%	May 15,	1975	1985
3¼%	June 15,	1978	1983
4%	Feb. 15,		1980
3½%	Nov. 15,		1980
3¼%	May 15,		1980
4¼%	August 15,	1987	1992
4%	Feb. 15,	1988	1993
4⅛%	May 15,	1989	1994
3½%	Feb. 15,		1990
3%	Feb. 15,		1995
3½%	Nov. 15,		1998

4

Should You Loan Your Money to Federal Agencies by Purchasing Agency Securities?

FEDERAL AGENCY SECURITIES

Congress creates hundreds of federal agencies to perform different jobs for the U.S. government. You know about certain federal agencies like the FBI or the CIA. However, there are over two dozen agencies you probably have never heard of whose job is to raise money and then reloan it to needy sectors of the U.S. economy. Whenever new needs for credit develop in the economy, Congress creates new agencies—to make loans for farm programs, to refinance home mortgages, to encourage community development, to help small businesses or to give aid to college students.

Federal agencies raise the money they reloan by selling federal agency securities. Agency securities are time deposits similar to bank time deposits and Treasury securities. When you buy agency securities, you are loaning a minimum of $1,000 (more often $5,000 or

$10,000 is required) to a particular agency for a specific period of time varying from months to over twenty years. The federal agency pays you interest for the use of your money and repays the face value of its securities when they come due, but generally not before they come due. If you need money for agency securities before maturity, you can borrow against them (use them as collateral) at a bank or you can sell them with their remaining maturities to other investors in the Government Securities Market, just as you would sell secondhand Treasury securities (see page 77). However, secondhand agency securities do not trade as actively as secondhand Treasury securities, and as a result, they bring relatively lower market resale prices if sold before maturity.

Some agency securities are indirectly guaranteed by the U.S. government (that is, if the agency cannot pay interest or repay the face value of its securities, the U.S. government will); however, most agency securities are guaranteed by the credit and the assets of the agency itself. Since all federal agencies are created by Congress and operate under a federal charter with government supervision, many investors believe Congress would never allow a federal agency to default on its securities.

Agency securities are attractive investments because they are considered safe and yet they pay ¼% to 1% more annual income than "like" Treasury securities. In other words, agency securities pay $2.50 to $10 a year more income on every $1,000 you invest than do Treasury securities with the same maturities. Furthermore, 1975 agency securities paid up to 2% more than "like" bank time deposits, or $20 more income a year for every $1,000 you invested.

New and secondhand agency securities are bought and sold at major commercial banks and large brokerage firms. You usually pay a service fee of about $25 to buy or sell agency securities in amounts of less than

$100,000, but there is generally no charge for large amounts. Naturally, if you pay a service charge, your yield is reduced.

When you loan money to a federal agency by purchasing its securities, you receive the agency's bond (its promise) to repay you on maturity date. Although agency securities offer various original maturity dates, they are usually called bonds no matter when they originally come due. In other words, they do not have specific names which identify their original maturity dates (like Treasury bills, notes and bonds). Federal agencies sell bonds that originally come due in a short time (one year or less), in a medium period of time (one to ten years) or in a long time (over ten years). We will discuss a few of the more popularly traded agency securities as well as the Federal Financing Bank, which is authorized to sell securities for many different federal agencies and to borrow money for them from the Treasury.

Short-Term Agency Securities
Two of the most actively traded agency securities that originally come due in less than one year are six-month agency bonds sold by the Banks for Cooperatives (Banks for Co-ops) and nine-month agency bonds sold by the Federal Intermediate Credit Banks (FICB) at the beginning of every month. They originally sell for their face value ($5,000 minimum) and pay interest at maturity in addition to the repayment of their face value. These short-term agency bonds are generally held for safekeeping at the bank or brokerage firm where they are purchased because they are issued only with bearer certificates and must be safeguarded as if they were cash (like T-bills, see page 63).

You buy six-month and nine-month agency time deposits for the same reasons you buy T-bills (see page 63). But short-term agency securities offer additional advantages over T-bills: You can buy them for a minimum of $5,000, whereas T-bills cost a minimum of about $10,000; they pay ¼% to ½% more annual interest than "like" T-bills. Furthermore, in 1975, they paid up to 8% annual interest (interest that is worth more than 8% because it is exempt from state and local income taxes), whereas six- or nine-month bank time deposits paid only 5¼% to 5¾% annual interest.

The Bank for Co-Ops and the FICB are two of the "Big 5" federal agencies, which are five of the biggest and oldest agencies selling securities. Their securities are guaranteed only by the credit and the assets of the particular agency issuing them. Although most "Big 5" agencies are made up of banks, these banks do not perform regular banking services. Instead, the thirteen Banks for Co-ops, the twelve FICB and the twelve Federal Land Banks (FLB), which are located throughout the United States, raise money by selling their securities and then reloan this money through their banks to farmers. The other two "Big 5" agencies—the twelve Federal Home Loan Banks (FHLB) and the Federal National Mortgage Association (Fannie Mae)—raise money by selling securities and then use this money to buy existing mortgages from banks and other lending institutions. In that way they make more money available for new mortgages.

Medium-Term Agency Securities

The most actively traded medium-term agency securities are also sold by a "Big 5" agency—the Federal Land Banks. Four to six times a year, Federal Land Banks sell bonds that originally come due in one to four years. These bonds originally sell for their $1,000 face value and pay interest separately twice a year. Since they offer the choice of coupon or registered certificate, interest is paid by either coupon or check.

You should buy Federal Land Bank bonds for the

same reason you buy Treasury notes (see page 65).
Even though Federal Land Banks securities pay ¼% to
½% more annual interest than Treasury notes, you
generally receive a higher yield by purchasing Treasury notes. Why? Because if you buy less than $100,000
worth of Federal Land Bank bonds the $25 service
charge you pay usually reduces your yield by more than
the additional ¼% to ½% interest they pay. On the
other hand, when you buy Treasury notes directly from
Federal Reserve Banks, you pay no charge and so your
yield is not reduced. Shop and compare yields and be
sure to deduct any charges you pay. In 1975, it was
more profitable to buy Federal Land Bank bonds than
to deposit money in bank time deposits even after deducting the $25 service charge because Federal Land
Bank securities paid up to 2% more annual interest
than "like" bank time deposits. Furthermore, Federal
Land Bank bond interest is exempt from state and local
income taxes, which makes it worth even more.

Long-Term Agency Securities
The Government National Mortgage Association (Ginnie Mae) sells actively traded long-term agency securities coming due in up to forty years. Ginnie Mae buys
existing mortgages from banks, other lending institutions and federal agencies and raises money by reselling shares of these mortgages to the investing public.
Ginnie Mae securities are indirectly guaranteed by the
U.S. government—if Ginnie Mae cannot pay the interest or repay the face value of its securities, the U.S.
government will. Furthermore, Ginnie Mae securities
usually pay a higher rate of interest than other agency
securities. Their interest, however, is not exempt from
state and local income taxes.

Ginnie Mae sells conventional long-term time deposits (like Treasury bonds) which originally mature in up
to twenty-five years. They are issued with coupon or

registered certificates and originally sell for their face value ($5,000 minimum). They pay interest separately twice a year by coupon or check and sometimes have a call provision (see page 66).

Ginnie Mae also sells unconventional long-term securities called pass-throughs, which are issued with only registered certificates. They originally sell for their face value ($25,000 minimum) and originally come due in thirty to forty years. What makes them unconventional is they pay both interest and return small amounts of their face value (principal) every month. In other words, when pass-throughs come due, there is nothing left to repay since the face value has been repaid before maturity by monthly payments. This repayment of the face value along with the interest every month means you receive much higher monthly payments than you would receive from interest alone. Therefore, pass-throughs offer a safe, monthly income (guaranteed by the U.S. government) which can be particularly useful for older people who want to reinvest money they have received from retirement funds and who do not object to the return of the face value of these securities before maturity.

You may wonder why they are called pass-throughs. Pass-through securities represent shares in million-dollar pools of home mortgages, and the monthly mortgage payments made by homeowners "pass through" to the owners of these securities. Since pass-through securities are guaranteed by the U.S. government, if the homeowners do not make their monthly payments, Uncle Sam makes them to the owners of the securities. And if the homeowners prepay mortgages (or if mortgages are foreclosed), these prepayments also "pass through" to the owners of pass-through securities. Although it is impossible to predict mortgage prepayments in any one mortgage pool, past experience indi-

cates the average life of a thirty-year pass-through security is approximately twelve years.

The Federal Financing Bank

The Federal Financing Bank (FFB) was created by
Congress to reduce the government's cost of borrowing
in the securities market. Instead of each small federal
agency (whose securities are guaranteed by the U.S.
government) selling its own securities, the FFB sells
one large issue of securities to raise the money for them.
The FFB can sell short-term securities (like T-bills),
medium-term securities (like Treasury notes) and long-
term securities (like Treasury bonds). All securities sold
by the FFB are guaranteed by the U.S. government.
The FFB is also authorized to borrow up to $5 billion
from the U.S. Treasury, and sometimes, rather than
selling securities, the FFB borrows the money these
agencies need from the Treasury.

In 1974, the FFB auctioned $1.5 billion of Federal
Financing Bank bills through Federal Reserve Banks
(the same way Treasury securities are auctioned, see
page 67). The FFB bills auctioned were eight-month
$10,000 time deposits with all the same characteristics
as Treasury bills, and yet the marketplace required
FFB bills to pay slightly higher yields than "like" Treasury bills. As a result, in 1975, rather than selling securities, the FFB borrowed the money these agencies
needed directly from the Treasury.

Despite the fact that many of the federal agencies
now borrowing through the FFB no longer sell new
securities, their secondhand securities (issued before
the FFB was established) still trade in the Government Securities Market. These secondhand securities
do not trade actively, which makes them more difficult to resell. As a result, they pay higher yields than
you would otherwise be able to receive from "like"
securities with a U.S. government guarantee. Should

you decide to buy these securities, do plan to keep them to maturity.

Buying and Selling New and Secondhand Agency Securities

Most federal agencies do not sell their securities directly to the investing public. Instead, they have business managers (fiscal agents) in New York City that set up a nationwide sales group consisting of banks, brokerage firms and security dealers. New agency securities are sold to members of this sales group for less than their listed price, and the sales group then resells them to the investing public for their listed price and makes a small profit.

Although banks and brokerage firms do not charge you a commission if you buy new agency securities in amounts of $100,000 or more, they do charge a service fee of about $25 if you buy them in smaller amounts. When banks and brokerage firms buy or sell secondhand agency securities for you, they make a commission (the difference between the bid and asked market prices), and they also charge a service fee on purchases or sales of less than $100,000. These commissions and charges vary and should be checked before placing an order.

Advance notice for new agency securities being sold appear publicly as news items and as advertisements in the *Wall Street Journal* and in the financial section of many city newspapers. On September 17, 1975, you could have read the following ad:

THE TWELVE FEDERAL
INTERMEDIATE CREDIT BANKS
$438,500,000   7.70% Consolidated Bonds
CUSIP No. 901174 BP 6
Dated October 1, 1975   Due July 1, 1976
Interest payable with principal at maturity
Price 100%

This is an ad for securities of the twelve Federal Intermediate Credit Banks—$438.5 million of new nine-month bonds dated October 1, 1975, which come due nine months later on July 1, 1976. You can buy them that day (September 17) at your bank or brokerage firm for 100% of their face value (at par), and you will receive fixed interest at a rate of 7.70% annually (less a $25 purchase charge if you buy less than $100,000 worth). You pay for these notes on October 1, the date your interest begins. This interest is paid to you at maturity at the same time the agency repays the face value (principal). The numbers after CUSIP (Committee on Uniform Security Identification Procedures) identify the particular offering of securities. You can find out their minimum price is $5,000 by checking the individual account for Federal Intermediate Credit Bank securities included at the end of this chapter (page 116).

These securities begin trading as secondhand agency securities in the Government Securities Market the day after this advertisement appears in the paper, and their prices move up and down as interest rates fluctuate (like secondhand Treasury securities, see page 77). You can follow the market prices of secondhand agency securities in the *Wall Street Journal* listed under the heading—Government, Agency and Miscellaneous Securities. Their secondhand prices are listed the same as the market prices of secondhand Treasury securities (see page 82). If secondhand agency securities pay interest by selling for less than their face value, they trade like secondhand T-bills (see page 77); and if they pay interest separately at maturity, by coupon or check, they trade like secondhand Treasury notes and bonds (see page 77).

The MY CASH Checklist for Agency Securities
The MY CASH checklist (see page 46) is helpful in determining when agency securities are the better buy.

Agency securities vary in minimum price from $1,000 to $100,000. They offer *M*aturity dates from days to forty years, which can be selected to fit your needs (see page 15). Their *Y*ields are increased if the interest paid by agency securities is exempt from state and local income taxes (not all interest on agency securities is exempt). In addition, their yields are worth more if they pay interest monthly or quarterly rather than semiannually or annually because the sooner you receive your interest, the sooner you can reinvest it to produce more income. Long-term agency securities are sometimes *C*allable at a price above face value. You can *A*nticipate a profit or loss if you sell agency securities with original maturities of over one year before maturity. You can anticipate a profit if they yield more than new ones and a loss if they yield less than new ones. The *S*afety of agency securities depends on their guarantee; those guaranteed by the U.S. government are safer than those guaranteed only by the agency itself. *H*ow much liquidity depends on how actively the particular agency securities trade. The less securities trade, the larger the commission a bank or brokerage firm charges. In other words, there is a larger difference between their bid and asked market prices (referred to as the spread). Of course, the larger the commission you pay, the less cash you receive if you sell agency securities before maturity.

Shirley Wright's New Role—Investment Shopper

After Shirley Wright reads about federal agency securities, she glances through all their individual accounts. There are so many agencies and so many different securities that she is confused.

As she closes her book, she hears the clock chiming 5 o'clock, time to head for the supermarket. She wants to take advantage of the advertised specials—5¢ off on the highest quality canned tuna fish, 7¢ off on her favorite brand of coffee and 3¢ off on the finest facial tissue. As she waits in the supermarket checkout line, she smiles to herself. If she can remember the prices and quality of dozens of grocery items, she ought to be able to learn what two dozen agency securities offer her. Actually, grocery shopping and investment shopping have the same goal: buying the highest quality at the best price.

Shirley begins to watch the ads for new agency securities on the financial page of her city newspaper. After several months, the names and yields of many agency securities start to become familiar. Then she checks their minimum prices, their safety and their liquidity in their individual accounts included at the end of this chapter. Soon she feels comfortable with agency securities.

Since Shirley has savings she can withdraw without a penalty (passbook savings account and U.S. savings bonds) and savings she can turn into cash easily (Treasury notes), she now will consider investing in agency securities that pay higher yields. She will not need this money before maturity so the lower market resale prices of agency securities will not be a disadvantage.

She calls her banker and broker to find out the yields for available agency securities and Treasury securities costing about $5,000 and coming due in four years or less. After comparing what they offered by using the MY CASH checklist, she concludes the best buy, at that time, is $5,000 worth of secondhand agency securities (guaranteed by the U.S. government) maturing in three years and yielding 8½%. These agency securities offer unequaled safety and yet pay $100 more income in three years than "like" Treasury securities and $300 more income than "like" bank time deposits if held to maturity, which Shirley plans to do. She decides to buy these agency securities. She still saves pennies on food bargains, but she also earns extra dollars on safe invest-ment bargains—*she is surely right.*

Individual accounts of agency securities follow. The "Big 5" agencies as well as agencies eligible to borrow through the Federal Financing Bank are identified at the top of each account. Although you will notice agency securities are called notes, bills, consolidated bonds, pass-throughs, debentures, participation certifi-cates and mortgaged-backed bonds, do not be in-timidated by these technical names; they are all time deposits of federal agencies, similar to bank time depos-its and Treasury securities.

Outlines of the three international agency securities follow those of federal agency securities. International agency securities are sponsored by many nations and are sold to raise money for needy or underdeveloped countries. They do not have a U.S. government guaran-tee, only the guarantee of the international agency it-self. These securities are not easily resold because their trading is relatively limited.

BANKS FOR COOPERATIVES (CO-OPS)
SECURITIES*
("Big 5" Agency)

Type of Security

IOUs of the 13 Banks for Co-ops—6-month bonds have bearer certificates; longer-term bonds have coupon certificates.

Type of Agency

An agency that makes loans to farm corporations.

Face or Par Values (Minimum)

$5,000.

Where to Buy, Sell and Redeem

At commercial banks or brokerage firms for a charge of about $25; there is usually no charge for trades of $100,000 or more. There is never a redemption charge. These charges can vary and should be checked before an order is placed.

Maturity Dates (New Securities)

6-month consolidated bonds are sold regularly every month with occasional longer maturities such as 2 to 5 years.

Yield (Minimum— 1975)

8.30% 6-month consolidated bonds pay interest at maturity; longer-term bonds pay interest semiannually. Interest is exempt from state and local income taxes.

*C*all Provision	Not callable.
*A*nticipated Profit or Loss (other than interest income)	The tax status of 6-month bonds treats gains or losses as interest income—never a profit or loss—but longer-term bonds can be sold for a profit if they yield more than new ones and sold for a loss if they yield less than new ones.
*S*afety	The repayment of their face value as well as their interest is guaranteed by the agency.
*H*ow Much Liquidity?	Securities can be sold for cash every trading day but do not trade as actively as Treasury securities. As a result, their market resale prices are usually lower than those of like Treasury securities. They can be borrowed against at a commercial bank for at least 1% above the current prime rate.

*All 37 Credit Banks, which include the 13 Banks for Co-ops, the 12 FICBs and the 12 FLBs, sell $50,000 discount notes that mature in 5 to 150 days at the discretion of the buyer.

COMMUNITY DEVELOPMENT
CORPORATION (CDC) SECURITIES
(Eligible to Borrow through the Federal
Financing Bank)

Type of Security	IOUs of the CDC—registered certificates.
Type of Agency	An agency that finances land acquisition and land development for new community projects.
Face or Par Values (Minimum)	$5,000.
Where to Buy, Sell and Redeem	New debentures bought at brokerage firms without a commission charge; old debentures usually bought or sold at brokerage firms on a net yield basis (which means the brokerage firm has taken its commission before the yield is quoted to you). There is never a redemption charge. These charges can vary and should be checked before an order is placed.
Maturity Dates (New Securities)	Debentures—up to 20 years.
Yield (Maximum—1975)	9%. Interest is paid semiannually.
Call Provision	Sometimes callable.

Anticipated Profit or Loss (other than interest income)	Anticipated profit if the securities are sold before maturity and yield more than new ones; anticipated loss if the securities sold yield less than new ones.
Safety	The repayment of their face value as well as their interest is guaranteed by the agency and indirectly guaranteed by the U.S. government.
How Much Liquidity?	Securities can be sold for cash every trading day but do not trade actively. As a result, their market resale prices are usually lower than those of Treasury securities or "Big 5" agency securities with similar maturities. They can be borrowed against at a commercial bank for at least 1% above the current prime rate.

DISTRICT OF COLUMBIA ARMORY
BOARD SECURITIES

Type of Security	IOUs of the D.C. Armory Board—registered certificates.
Type of Agency	An agency to finance the construction and operation of the stadium in Washington, D.C., to July 1, 1990.
Face or Par Values (Minimum)	$10,000.
Where to Buy, Sell and Redeem	At commercial banks or brokerage firms for a charge of about $25; there is usually no charge for trades of $100,000 or more. There is never a redemption charge. These charges can vary and should be checked before an order is placed.
Maturity Dates (New Securities)	Bonds—up to 20 years.
Yield (Maximum— 1975)*	Interest is paid semiannually.
Call Provision	Sometimes callable.
Anticipated Profit or Loss (other than interest income)	Anticipated profit if the securities are sold before maturity and yield more than new ones; anticipated loss if the securities sold yield less than new ones.

Safety

The repayment of their face value as well as their interest is guaranteed by the agency and indirectly guaranteed by the U.S. government.

How Much Liquidity?

Securities can be sold for cash every trading day but do not trade actively. As a result, their market resale prices are usually lower than those of Treasury securities or "Big 5" agency securities with similar maturities. They can be borrowed against at a commercial bank for at least 1% above the current prime rate.

*Figures not available for 1975.

EXPORT-IMPORT BANK (EXIM BANK)
SECURITIES
(Eligible to Borrow through the Federal Financing Bank)

Type of Security	IOUs of the EXIM Bank— coupon or registered certificates.
Type of Agency	An agency that makes loans to American and foreign firms to encourage trade.
Face or Par Values (Minimum)	$5,000.
Where to Buy, Sell and Redeem	At commercial banks or brokerage firms for a charge of about $25; there is usually no charge for trades of $100,000 or more. There is never a redemption charge. These charges can vary and should be checked before an order is placed.
Maturity Dates (New Securities)	Bonds—3 to 7 years. Participation certificates—to 20 years.
Yield (Maximum— 1975)	8.45%. Interest is paid semiannually.
Call Provision	Not callable.

*A*nticipated Profit or Loss (other than interest income)	Anticipated profit if the securities are sold before maturity and yield more than new ones; anticipated loss if the securities sold yield less than new ones.
*S*afety	The repayment of the face value and interest of the bonds are guaranteed by the agency as well as by the U.S. government. The repayment of the face value and interest of participation certificates is sometimes guaranteed only by the agency, whereas at other times it is guaranteed by the agency as well as the U.S. government.
*H*ow Much Liquidity?	Securities can be sold for cash every trading day but do not trade as actively as Treasury securities. As a result, their market resale prices are slightly lower than those of like Treasury securities. They can be borrowed against at a commercial bank for at least 1% above the current prime rate.

FARMERS HOME ADMINISTRATION (FHDA) SECURITIES
(Eligible to Borrow through the Federal Financing Bank)

Type of Security	IOUs of the FHDA—coupon or registered certificates.
Type of Agency	An agency that makes loans to individual farmers.
Face or Par Values (Minimum—1975)	Varies: $25,000, $50,000, $100,000, $500,000 or $1 million.
Where to Buy, Sell and Redeem	At commercial banks or brokerage firms for a charge of about $25; there is usually no charge for trades of $100,000 or more. There is never a redemption charge. These charges can vary and should be checked before an order is placed.
Maturity Dates (New Securities)	Insured notes—1 up to 25 years.
Yield (Maximum—1975)	8.81%. Interest is paid annually.
Call Provision	Sometimes callable.
Anticipated Profit or Loss (other than interest income)	Anticipated profit if the securities are sold before maturity and yield more than new ones; anticipated loss if the securities sold yield less than new ones.

*S*afety	The repayment of their face value as well as their interest is guaranteed by the agency and indirectly guaranteed by the U.S. government.
*H*ow Much Liquidity?	Securities can be sold for cash every trading day but do not trade actively. They are more difficult to sell because they have varying minimum purchase prices. As a result, their market resale prices are usually lower than those of like Treasury securities or "Big 5" agency securities. They can be borrowed against at a commercial bank for at least 1% above the current prime rate.

FEDERAL FINANCING BANK (FFB)
SECURITIES

Type of Security

IOUs of the FFB—bearer certificates.

Type of Agency

An agency to consolidate borrowing for many federal agencies and other borrowers whose obligations are guaranteed by the U.S. government.

Face or Par Values (Minimum)

Bills—$10,000.

Where to Buy, Sell and Redeem

New FFB bills bought at Federal Reserve Banks (no commission charge); new and old FFB bills bought and sold at banks or brokerage firms (charge about $25 and usually no charge for trades of $100,000 or more). There is never a redemption charge. These charges can vary and should be checked before an order is placed.

Maturity Dates (New Securities)

Only 1 issue to date (1975), which was sold in 1974 with a maturity date of 8 months.

*Y*ield (Maximum—1975)	The maximum yield on the 1 issue of FFB bills in 1974 was close to 10%. Interest was paid by selling for less than face value and was exempt from state and local income taxes.
*C*all Provision	Not callable.
*A*nticipated Profit or Loss (other than interest income)	The tax status of FFB bills treats gains or losses as interest income—never a profit or a loss. Therefore, we cannot anticipate a profit or loss.
*S*afety	The repayment of their face value as well as their interest is guaranteed by the FFB and also by the U.S. government.
*H*ow Much Liquidity?	Securities traded every trading day but not as actively as T-bills. As a result, their market resale prices were slightly lower than those of like T-bills. They could be borrowed against at a commercial bank for at least 1% above the current prime rate.

FEDERAL INTERMEDIATE CREDIT
BANKS (FICB) SECURITIES*
("Big 5" Agency)

Type of Security	IOUs of the 12 FICB— 9-month bonds have bearer certificates; longer-term bonds have coupon certificates.
Type of Agency	An agency that loans money to credit associations, which in turn make loans to farmers.
Face or Par Values (Minimum)	$5,000.
Where to Buy, Sell and Redeem	At commercial banks or brokerage firms for a charge of about $25; there is usually no charge for trades of $100,000 or more. There is never a redemption charge. These charges can vary and should be checked before an order is placed.
Maturity Dates (New Securities)	9-month consolidated bonds are sold regularly every month with occasional longer maturities such as 2 to 5 years.

Yield (Maximum— 1975)	8.43% 9-month consolidated bonds pay interest at maturity; longer-term bonds pay interest semiannually. Interest is exempt from state and local income taxes.
Call Provision	Not callable.
Anticipated Profit or Loss (other than interest income)	The tax status of 9-month bonds treats gains or losses as interest income—never a profit or loss—but longer-term bonds can be sold for a profit if they yield more than new ones and sold for a loss if they yield less than new ones.
Safety	The repayment of their face value as well as their interest is guaranteed by the agency.
How Much Liquidity?	Securities can be sold for cash every trading day but do not trade as actively as Treasury securities. As a result, their market resale prices are usually lower than those of like Treasury securities. They can be borrowed against at a commercial bank for at least 1% above the current prime rate.

*All 37 Farm Credit Banks, including the 12 FICB, sell $50,000 discount notes that mature in 5 to 150 days at the discretion of the buyer.

FEDERAL HOME LOAN BANKS (FHLB)
SECURITIES
("Big 5" Agency)

Type of Security

IOUs of the 12 FHLB—notes have bearer certificates; bonds have coupon certificates.

Type of Agency

An agency that loans money to S&Ls and institutions that make mortgage loans to home owners.

Face or Par Values (Minimum)

Notes and bonds—$10,000. Discount notes—$100,000.

Where to Buy, Sell and Redeem

At commercial banks or brokerage firms for a charge of about $25; there is usually no charge for trades of $100,000 or more. There is never a redemption charge. These charges can vary and should be checked before an order is placed.

Maturity Dates (New Securities)

Notes—under 1 year. Discount notes—30 to 360 days (buyer's discretion). Bonds—over 1 year.

Yield (Maximum— 1975)	8.67%. Notes pay interest at maturity; discount notes pay interest by selling for less than their face value; bonds pay interest semiannually. Interest is exempt from state and local income taxes.
Call Provision	Not callable.
Anticipated Profit or Loss (other than interest income)	The tax status of all notes treats gains or losses as interest income—never a profit or loss—but bonds can be sold for a profit if they yield more than new ones and sold for a loss if they yield less than new ones.
Safety	The repayment of their face value as well as their interest is guaranteed by the agency.
How Much Liquidity?	Securities can be sold for cash every trading day but do not trade as actively as Treasury securities. As a result, their market resale prices are usually lower than those of like Treasury securities. They can be borrowed against at a commercial bank for at least 1% above the current prime rate.

FEDERAL HOME LOAN MORTGAGE
CORPORATION (FHLMC) SECURITIES

Type of Security	IOUs of the FHLMC—coupon certificates.
Type of Agency	An agency that buys mortgages from the FHL Bank and other lending institutions and resells them to investors.
Face or Par Values (Minimum)	Participation certificates— $100,000. Mortgage-backed bonds—$25,000.
Where to Buy, Sell and Redeem	At commercial banks or brokerage firms for a charge of about $25; there is usually no charge for trades of $100,000 or more. There is never a redemption charge. These charges can vary and should be checked before an order is placed.
Maturity Dates (New Securities)	Participation certificates—up to 30 years. Mortgage-backed bonds—up to 25 years.
Yield (Maximum— 1975)	8.97%. Interest is paid semiannually.
Call Provision	Sometimes callable.

Anticipated Profit or Loss (other than interest income)	Anticipated profit if the securities are sold before maturity and yield more than new ones; anticipated loss if the securities sold yield less than new ones.
Safety	The repayment of the face value and interest of participation certificates are guaranteed by the agency. The repayment of the face value and interest of mortgage-backed bonds is guaranteed by Ginnie Mae, which automatically carries with it an indirect guarantee by the U.S. government.
How Much Liquidity?	Securities can be sold for cash every trading day but do not trade actively. As a result, their market resale prices are usually lower than those of Treasury securities or "Big 5" agency securities with similar maturities. They can be borrowed against at a commercial bank for at least 1% above the current prime rate.

FEDERAL HOUSING AUTHORITY (FHA) SECURITIES

Type of Security	IOUs of the FHA—registered certificates.
Type of Agency	An agency that insures mortgage loans for residential housing and resells them to investors.
Face or Par Values (Minimum)	$50 to $5,000.
Where to Buy, Sell and Redeem	At commercial banks or brokerage firms for a charge of about $25; there is usually no charge for trades of $100,000 or more. There is never a redemption charge. These charges can vary and should be checked before an order is placed.
Maturity Dates (New Securities)	Debentures—up to 20 years.
Yield (Maximum—1975)	8.43%. Interest is paid semiannually and is exempt from state and local income taxes.
Call Provision	Sometimes callable.
Anticipated Profit or Loss (other than interest income)	Anticipated profit if the securities are sold before maturity and yield more than new ones; anticipated loss if the securities sold yield less than new ones.

Safety

The repayment of their face value as well as their interest is guaranteed by the agency and indirectly guaranteed by the U.S. government.

How Much Liquidity?

Securities can be sold for cash every trading day but do not trade actively. As a result, their market resale prices are usually lower than those of Treasury securities or "Big 5" agency securities with similar maturities. They can be borrowed against at a commercial bank for at least 1% above the current prime rate.

FEDERAL LAND BANKS (FLB)
SECURITIES*
("Big 5" Agency)

Type of Security	IOUs of the 12 FLB—coupon certificates.
Type of Agency	An agency that makes long-term loans to farmers secured by first mortgages on farm real estate.
Face or Par Values (Minimum)	$1,000.
Where to Buy, Sell and Redeem	At commercial banks or brokerage firms for a charge of about $25 with usually no charge for trades of $100,000 or more. There is never a redemption charge. These charges can vary and should be checked before an order is placed.
Maturity Dates (New Securities)	Bonds—up to 15 years (usually sold 4 to 6 times a year).
Yield (Maximum—1975)	8.84%. Interest is paid semiannually and is exempt from state and local income taxes.
Call Provision	Recent issues have not been callable.

Anticipated Profit or Loss (other than interest income)	Anticipated profit if the securities are sold before maturity and yield more than new ones; anticipated loss if the securities sold yield less than new ones.
Safety	The repayment of their face value as well as their interest is guaranteed by the agency.
How Much Liquidity?	Securities can be sold for cash every trading day but do not trade as actively as Treasury securities. As a result, their market resale prices are usually lower than those of like Treasury securities. They can be borrowed against at a commercial bank for at least 1% above the current prime rate.

*All 37 Credit Banks, including the 12 Federal Land Banks, sell $50,000 discount notes that mature in 5 to 150 days at the discretion of the buyer.

FEDERAL NATIONAL MORTGAGE ASSOCIATION (FANNIE MAE) SECURITIES
("Big 5" Agency)

Type of Security	IOUs of Fannie Mae—coupon certificates.
Type of Agency	An agency that buys mortgages and resells them to investors.
Face or Par Values (Minimum)	Debentures—$10,000. Discount notes—$5,000. Mortgage-backed bonds—$25,000.
Where to Buy, Sell and Redeem	At commercial banks or brokerage firms for a charge of about $25; there is usually no charge for trades of $100,000 or more. There is never a redemption charge. These charges can vary and should be checked before an order is placed.
Maturity Dates (New Securities)	Debenture and mortgage-backed bonds—to 25 years. Debentures—25 years. Discount notes—30 to 270 days.

Yield (Maximum— 1975)	8.71%. Debentures and mortgage-backed bonds pay interest semiannually; discount notes pay interest by selling for less than their face value.
Call Provision	Not callable, but mortgage prepayments are allowable.
Anticipated Profit or Loss (other than interest income)	The tax status of discount notes treats gains or losses as interest income—never a profit or a loss—but mortgage-backed bonds and debentures can be sold for a profit if they yield more than new ones and sold for a loss if they yield less than new ones.
Safety	The repayment of the face value as well as the interest of discount notes and debentures is guaranteed by Fannie Mae. Mortgage-backed bonds are also guaranteed indirectly by the U.S. government.
How Much Liquidity?	Securities can be sold for cash every trading day but do not trade as actively as Treasury securities. As a result, their market resale prices are usually lower than those of like Treasury securities. They can be borrowed against at a commercial bank for at least 1% above the current prime rate.

GENERAL SERVICES ADMINISTRATION (GSA) SECURITIES
(Eligible to Borrow through the Federal Financing Bank)

Type of Security	IOUs of the GSA—registered certificates.
Type of Agency	An agency that finances the construction of federal building projects.
Face or Par Values (Minimum)	$5,000.
Where to Buy, Sell and Redeem	At commercial banks or brokerage firms for a charge of about $25 with usually no charge for trades of $100,000 or more. There is never a redemption charge. These charges can vary and should be checked before an order is placed.
Maturity Dates (New Securities)	Participation certificates—up to 30 years.
Yield (Maximum—1975)	8.84%. Interest is paid semiannually and is exempt from state and local income taxes.
Call Provision	Sometimes callable.

Anticipated Profit or Loss (other than interest income)	Anticipated profit if the securities are sold before maturity and yield more than new ones; anticipated loss if the securities sold yield less than new ones.
Safety	The repayment of their face value as well as their interest is guaranteed by the agency and indirectly guaranteed by the U.S. government.
How Much Liquidity?	Securities can be sold for cash every trading day but do not trade actively. As a result, their market resale prices are usually lower than those of Treasury securities or "Big 5" agency securities with similar maturities. They can be borrowed against at a commercial bank for at least 1% above the current prime rate.

GOVERNMENT NATIONAL MORTGAGE ASSOCIATION (GINNIE MAE) SECURITIES

Type of Security

IOUs of Ginnie Mae—coupon or registered certificates.

Type of Agency

An agency that guarantees mortgages issued by banks, other lending institutions or government agencies and resells them to investors.

Face or Par Values (Minimum)

Participation certificates—$5,000.
Mortgage-backed bonds—$25,000.
Pass-throughs—$25,000.

Where to Buy, Sell and Redeem

At commercial banks or brokerage firms for a charge of about $25; there is usually no charge for trades of $100,000 or more. There is never a redemption charge. These charges can vary and should be checked before an order is placed.

Maturity Dates (New Securities)

Participation certificates—8 to 25 years.
Mortgage-backed bonds—1 to 25 years.
Pass-throughs—12 to 40 years.

Yield (Maximum—1975)	9.08%. Participation certificates and mortgage-backed bonds pay interest semiannually; pass-throughs pay interest monthly.
Call Provision	Not callable, but mortgage prepayments are allowable.
Anticipated Profit or Loss (other than interest income)	Anticipated profit if the securities are sold before maturity and yield more than new ones; anticipated loss if the securities sold yield less than new ones.
Safety	The repayment of their face value as well as their interest is guaranteed by the agency and indirectly guaranteed by the U.S. government.
How Much Liquidity?	Securities can be sold for cash every trading day but do not trade as actively as Treasury securities. As a result, their market resale prices are usually lower than those of like Treasury securities. They can be borrowed against for at least 1% above the current prime rate.

MARITIME ADMINISTRATION
SECURITIES
(Eligible to Borrow from the Federal Financing Bank)

Type of Security

IOUs of the Maritime Administration—registered certificates.

Type of Agency

An agency that finances the construction of new ships.

Face or Par Values (Minimum)

$1,000.

Where to Buy, Sell and Redeem

New bonds bought at brokerage firms without a commission charge; old bonds usually bought or sold at brokerage firms on a net yield basis. There is never a redemption charge. These charges can vary and should be checked before an order is placed.

Maturity Dates (New Securities)

Bonds—up to 25 years.

Yield (Maximum—1975)

9.31%. Interest is paid semiannually.

Call Provision

Sometimes callable.

Anticipated Profit or Loss (other than interest income)

Anticipated profit if the securities are sold before maturity and yield more than new ones; anticipated loss if the securities sold yield less than new ones.

Safety	The repayment of their face value as well as their interest is guaranteed by the agency and indirectly guaranteed by the U.S. government.
How Much Liquidity?	Securities can be sold for cash every trading day but do not trade actively. As a result, their market resale prices are usually lower than those of Treasury securities or "Big 5" agency securities with similar maturities. They can be borrowed against at a commercial bank for at least 1% above the current prime rate.

SMALL BUSINESS ADMINISTRATION
(SBA) SECURITIES
(Eligible to Borrow through the Federal
Financing Bank)

Type of Security	IOUs of the SBA—registered certificates.
Type of Agency	An agency that furnishes financial and management assistance to small businesses.
Face or Par Values (Minimum)	$10,000.
Where to Buy, Sell and Redeem	At commercial banks or brokerage firms for a charge of about $25; there is usually no charge for trades of $100,000 or more. There is never a redemption charge. These charges can vary and should be checked before an order is placed.
Maturity Dates (New Securities)	Debentures—up to 15 years.
Yield (Maximum— 1975)	8.65%. Interest is paid semiannually and is exempt from state and local income taxes.
Call Provision	Not callable.

Anticipated Profit or Loss (other than interest income)	Anticipated profit if the securities are sold before maturity and yield more than new ones; anticipated loss if the securities sold yield less than new ones.
Safety	The repayment of their face value as well as their interest is guaranteed by the agency and indirectly guaranteed by the U.S. government.
How Much Liquidity?	Securities can be sold for cash every trading day but do not trade actively. As a result, their market resale prices are usually lower than those of Treasury securities or "Big 5" agency securities with similar maturities. They can be borrowed against at a commercial bank for at least 1% above the current prime rate.

STUDENT LOAN MARKETING ASSOCIATION (SALLIE MAE) SECURITIES
(Eligible to Borrow through the Federal Financing Bank)

Type of Security	IOUs of Sallie Mae—bearer certificates.
Type of Agency	An agency to help finance student loans.
Face or Par Values (Minimum)	$10,000.
Where to Buy, Sell and Redeem	At commercial banks or brokerage firms for a charge of about $25; there is usually no charge for trades of $100,000 or more. There is never a redemption charge. These charges can vary and should be checked before an order is placed.
Maturity Dates (New Securities)	Discount notes—six months.
Yield (Maximum— 1975)*	Interest is paid by selling for less than face value.
Call Provision	Not callable.
Anticipated Profit or Loss (other than interest income)	The tax status of discount notes treats gains or losses as interest income—never a profit or a loss. Therefore, we cannot anticipate a profit or loss.

Safety	The repayment of their face value as well as their interest is guaranteed by the agency. It is also indirectly guaranteed by the U.S. government if securities are issued before July 1, 1982.
How Much Liquidity?	Securities can be sold for cash every trading day but do not trade actively. As a result, their market resale prices are usually lower than those of Treasury securities or "Big 5" agency securities with similar maturities. They can be borrowed against at a commercial bank for at least 1% above the current prime rate.

*No figures available for 1975.

TENNESSEE VALLEY AUTHORITY (TVA) SECURITIES
(Eligible to Borrow through the Federal Financing Bank)

Type of Security

IOUs of the TVA—discount notes have bearer certificates; bonds have coupons or registered certificates.

Type of Agency

An agency to assist in the development of the resources of the Tennessee River basin.

Face or Par Values (Minimum)

Discount notes—$5,000. Bonds—$1,000.

Where to Buy, Sell and Redeem

At commercial banks or brokerage firms for a charge of about $25; there is usually no charge for trades of $100,000 or more. There is never a redemption charge. These charges can vary and should be checked before an order is placed.

Maturity Dates (New Securities)

Discount notes—4 months. Bonds—up to 25 years.

Yield (Maximum— 1975)

8.99%. Notes pay interest by selling for less than their face value; bonds pay interest semiannually. This interest is exempt from state and local income taxes.

Call Provision	Discount notes—not callable. Bonds—sometimes callable.
Anticipated Profit or Loss (other than interest income)	The tax status of discount notes treats gains or losses as interest income—never a profit or loss—but bonds can be sold for a profit if they yield more than new ones and sold for a loss if they yield less than new ones.
Safety	The repayment of their face value as well as their interest is guaranteed only by the net TVA power proceeds received.
How Much Liquidity?	Securities can be sold for cash every trading day but do not trade actively. As a result, their market resale prices are usually lower than those of Treasury securities or "Big 5" agency securities with similar maturities. They can be borrowed against at a commercial bank for at least 1% above the current prime rate.

U.S. POSTAL SERVICE SECURITIES
(Eligible to Borrow through the Federal Financing Bank)

Type of Security	IOUs of the U.S. Postal Service—coupon or registered certificates.
Type of Agency	An agency to finance the capital expenditures and current operations of the U.S. Postal Service.
Face or Par Values (Minimum)	$10,000.
Where to Buy, Sell and Redeem	At commercial banks or brokerage firms for a charge of about $25; there is usually no charge for trades of $100,000 or more. There is never a redemption charge. These charges can vary and should be checked before an order is placed.
Maturity Dates (New Securities)	Bonds—up to 25 years.
Yield (Maximum— 1975)	8.94%. Interest is paid semiannually and is exempt from state and local income taxes.
Call Provision	Sometimes callable.

Anticipated Profit or Loss (other than interest income)	Anticipated profit if the securities are sold before maturity and yield more than new ones; anticipated loss if the securities sold yield less than new ones.
Safety	The repayment of their face value as well as their interest is guaranteed by the assets, revenues and receipts of the Postal Service. Postal securities can also be indirectly guaranteed by the U.S. government if the Postal Service asks for this guarantee at the time of issue.
How Much Liquidity?	Securities can be sold for cash every trading day but do not trade actively. As a result, their market resale prices are usually lower than those of Treasury securities or "Big 5" agency securities with similar maturities. They can be borrowed against at a commercial bank for at least 1% above the current prime rate.

WASHINGTON METROPOLITAN AREA TRANSIT AUTHORITY SECURITIES
(Eligible to Borrow through the Federal Financing Bank)

Type of Security	IOUs of the Washington Metropolitan Area Transit Authority—coupon or registered certificates.
Type of Agency	An agency to help plan, develop and provide for the operation of mass transit facilities serving the Washington, D.C., metropolitan area.
Face or Par Values (Minimum)	$5,000.
Where to Buy, Sell and Redeem	At commercial banks or brokerage firms for a charge of about $25; there is usually no charge for trades of $100,000 or more. There is never a redemption charge. These charges can vary and should be checked before an order is placed.
Maturity Dates (New Securities)	Bonds—up to 40 years.

Yield (Maximum—1975)	8.80%. Interest is paid semiannually and may or may not be exempt from state or local income taxes. Owner should check the taxing authority of the specific state.
Call Provision	Sometimes callable.
Anticipated Profit or Loss (other than interest income)	Anticipated profit if the securities are sold before maturity and yield more than new ones; anticipated loss if the securities sold yield less than new ones.
Safety	The repayment of their face value as well as their interest is guaranteed by the agency and indirectly guaranteed by the U.S. government.
How Much Liquidity?	Securities can be sold for cash every trading day but do not trade actively. As a result, their market resale prices are usually lower than those of Treasury securities or "Big 5" agency securities with similar maturities. They can be borrowed against at a commercial bank for at least 1% above the current prime rate.

ASIAN DEVELOPMENT BANK (ADB)
SECURITIES
(International Agency)

Type of Security — IOUs of the ADB—registered certificates.

Type of Agency — 37 governments make loans to foster economic growth in Asia and the Far East.

Face or Par Values (Minimum) — $1,000.

Where to Buy, Sell and Redeem — At commercial banks or brokerage firms for a charge of about $25; there is usually no charge for trades of $100,000 or more. There is never a redemption charge. These charges can vary and should be checked before an order is placed.

Maturity Dates (New Securities) — Notes—up to 5 years. Bonds—up to 25 years.

Yield (Maximum— 1975) — 8.74%. Interest is paid semiannually.

Call Provision — Sometimes callable.

Anticipated Profit or Loss (other than interest income) — Anticipated profit if the securities are sold before maturity and yield more than new ones; anticipated loss if the securities sold yield less than new ones.

Safety	The repayment of their face value as well as their interest is guaranteed only by the ADB.
How Much Liquidity?	Securities are not easily sold because of limited trading. They can also be borrowed against at commercial banks.

INTER-AMERICAN DEVELOPMENT
BANK (I-ADB) SECURITIES
(International Agency)

Type of Security	IOUs of the I-ADB—registered certificates.
Type of Agency	24 governments make loans for economic development in Latin America.
Face or Par Values (Minimum)	$1,000.
Where to Buy, Sell and Redeem	At commercial banks or brokerage firms for a charge of about $25; there is usually no charge for trades of $100,000 or more. There is never a redemption charge. These charges can vary and should be checked before an order is placed.
Maturity Dates (New Securities)	Bonds—up to 25 years.
Yield (Maximum—1975)	8.78%. Interest is paid semiannually.
Call Provision	Sometimes callable.
Anticipated Profit or Loss (other than interest income)	Anticipated profit if the securities are sold before maturity and yield more than new ones; anticipated loss if the securities sold yield less than new ones.

*S*afety	The repayment of their face value as well as their interest is guaranteed only by the I-ADB.
*H*ow Much Liquidity?	Securities are not easily sold because of limited trading. They can also be borrowed against at commercial banks.

INTERNATIONAL BANK FOR RECONSTRUCTION & DEVELOPMENT (WORLD BANK) SECURITIES
(International Agency)

Type of Security	IOUs of the World Bank—registered certificates.
Types of Agency	122 member nations make loans to governments and private organizations in underdeveloped countries.
Face or Par Values (Minimum)	$1,000.
Where to Buy, Sell and Redeem	At commercial banks or brokerage firms for a charge of about $25; there is usually no charge for trades of $100,000 or more. There is never a redemption charge. These charges can vary and should be checked before an order is placed.
Maturity Dates (New Securities)	Bonds—up to 25 years.
Yield (Maximum— 1975)	8.79%. Interest is paid semiannually.
Call Provision	Sometimes callable.
Anticipated Profit or Loss (other than interest income)	Anticipated profit if the securities are sold before maturity and yield more than new ones; anticipated loss if the securities sold yield less than new ones.

| Safety | The repayment of their face value as well as their interest is guaranteed only by the World Bank. |
| How Much Liquidity? | Securities are not easily sold because of limited trading. They can also be borrowed against at commercial banks. |

5

Should You Loan Your Money to Municipalities by Purchasing Municipal Notes? Municipal Bonds?

MUNICIPAL SECURITIES

In 1975, New York City became "Trouble City" instead of "Fun City" because it was having trouble repaying its debts—its municipal securities. However, not all municipal securities are threatened with default. There are over 50,000 different municipal securities, many of which are safe, some even guaranteed by the U.S. government. But what are municipal securities? They are time deposits sold by all governments other than the federal government, such as states, territories and cities, as well as their agencies and authorities. Why do they sell municipal securities? To raise billions of dollars for needed major local projects such as schools, hospitals, airports, highways, power plants or sewage systems.

150

You can loan a minimum of $1,000 (although more often $5,000 is required) to a particular municipality for a period of months to over forty years by purchasing its municipal securities at banks or brokerage firms. The municipality pays you annual interest and repays the face value of its securities at maturity, but not before maturity (unless there is a call provision). If you want the money for municipal securities before they come due, you can borrow against them, or you can sell them with their remaining maturities in the Municipal Securities Market similar to the way secondhand Treasury securities are sold in the Government Securities Market (see page 77). Since municipal securities do not trade as actively as Treasury securities, they bring relatively lower market resale prices. Thus, whenever possible, municipal securities should be held to maturity.

There are major differences between municipal securities and Treasury securities. Most important is that the interest paid by municipal securities is exempt from federal income tax (tax-free). This federal tax exemption dates back to 1819 when the Supreme Court ruled that the U.S. government could not tax state obligations because the power to tax was the power to destroy, and that therefore neither the state nor the federal government should have the power to destroy each other. That is also the reason why interest paid by U.S. government securities is exempt from state and local taxes.

When investors do not have to pay federal income tax on the interest they receive, they are willing to accept lower rates of interest. This works to the benefit of municipalities because they save money by paying lower interest rates, and also to the benefit of investors because they keep more money by not paying taxes on the interest they receive. For example, if you are in a 50% tax bracket, 5% tax-free interest is more profitable for you than 8% taxable interest. Why? Because you

keep 100% of the 5% tax-free interest, but you only
keep 50% of the 8% taxable interest (or 4%) since the
other 50% goes to Uncle Sam for taxes. Furthermore,
if you buy municipal securities sold by your home state,
the District of Columbia, Puerto Rico, the Virgin Islands or Guam, as well as by their agencies and authorities, the interest paid by these municipal securities is
exempt from state and local income taxes too.

Naturally, the higher your tax bracket, the more valuable tax-free interest becomes. You can use the table
on page 154 to determine if, in your tax bracket, tax-
free yields paid currently are more or less profitable
than taxable yields being paid. In general, when your
taxable income is $18,000 or more, you should consider
buying municipal securities.

Are Municipal Securities Safe Investments?
For years, municipal securities were considered second
in safety to U.S. government securities; however, this is
no longer true. Why? Because some municipalities are
having financial problems. They have been spending
beyond their means and are now having difficulty
repaying their debts. Since municipal governments
cannot print money (like the U.S. government), they
must default when they cannot repay debts. In 1974,
there were several defaults on municipal securities, but
the public's first awareness was when the New York
State Urban Development Corporation defaulted on
over $800 million worth of municipal securities. Al-
though many investors believed that if municipalities
were ever in financial trouble, the U.S. government
would certainly bail them out, it did not come to the aid
of the New York Urban Development Corporation.

Today, investors are more cautious about buying municipal securities. They want to select securities more
likely to be repaid under all circumstances. Since it is
difficult to analyze the financial statements of munici-

pal securities, investors usually judge the safety of these securities by the quality ratings of independent advisory services such as Moody Investor Service (Moody's) and Standard & Poor (S&P), whose business it is to analyze and to rate various marketable securities, including municipal securities. Moody's and S&P ratings start, respectively, with Aaa or AAA (highest quality or safest) going to Aa or AA (high quality or probably safe) to A (medium quality) all the way to D (securities already in default). However, even rating services can make mistakes; for example, the New York State Urban Development Corporation bonds had an A rating when it defaulted on its notes.

As more and more investors became concerned about the safety of owning municipal securities, the Municipal Bond Insurance Association (MBIA) was established. The MBIA, which is composed of four of America's largest and best-known insurance companies, insures both the principal and interest payment of certain new issues of municipal securities. The MBIA guarantee adds additional safety to the ownership of municipal securities which, in turn, gives them higher ratings. Since the yields that municipal securities pay are commensurate with their risk, the higher the ratings, the lower the yields. You can telephone your bank or brokerage firm for the ratings and yields on the various municipal securities.

When you loan money to a municipality by purchasing municipal securities, you receive the municipality's bond (its promise) to repay you on maturity date. Municipal bonds that come due in less than one year are called municipal notes, and those that originally come due in more than one year are called municipal bonds.

Municipal Notes
Municipal notes are sold by municipalities to borrow cash for one year or less, usually in anticipation of tax

THE APPROXIMATE TAX-FREE INTEREST THAT
EQUALS THE TAXABLE YIELD IN YOUR TAX BRACKET

If Tax-Free Interest Is—			3.50	4.00	4.50	5.00	5.50	6.00	6.50	7.00
Your Tax Bracket	Your Taxable Income									
	SINGLE RETURN	JOINT RETURN	Taxable Yields Equal to Above Tax-Free Yields*							
36%	$18,000–$20,000	$24,000–$28,000	5.47	6.25	7.03	7.81	8.59	9.37	10.16	10.94
39%		$28,000–$32,000	5.74	6.56	7.38	8.20	9.02	9.84	10.66	11.48
40%	$20,000–$26,000		5.83	6.67	7.50	8.33	9.17	10.00	10.83	11.67
42%		$32,000–$36,000	6.03	6.90	7.76	8.62	9.48	10.34	11.21	12.07
45%	$26,000–$32,000	$36,000–$40,000	6.36	7.27	8.18	9.09	10.00	10.91	11.82	12.73
48%		$40,000–$44,000	6.73	7.69	8.65	9.62	10.58	11.54	12.50	13.46

	Income (joint)	Income (single)								
50%	$32,000–$38,000	$44,000–$52,000	7.00	8.00	9.00	10.00	11.00	12.00	13.00	14.00
53%		$52,000–$64,000	7.45	8.51	9.57	10.64	11.70	12.77	13.83	14.89
55%	$38,000–$44,000	$64,000–$76,000	7.78	8.89	10.00	11.11	12.22	13.33	14.44	15.56
58%	$76,000–$88,000		8.33	9.52	10.71	11.90	13.10	14.29	15.48	16.67
60%	$44,000–$50,000	$88,000–$100,000	8.75	10.00	11.25	12.50	13.75	15.00	16.25	17.50
62%	$50,000–$60,000	$100,000–$120,000	9.21	10.53	11.84	13.16	14.47	15.79	17.11	18.42

Yield figures © Merrill Lynch, Pierce, Fenner & Smith, Inc.
Reprinted by permission of Merrill Lynch, Pierce, Fenner & Smith, Inc., New York, N.Y.

*Not including possible savings from state and local income tax exemptions.

revenues or of selling long-term municipal bonds. Municipal notes range in minimum cost from $5,000 to $100,000 and originally come due in one year or less. They also originally sell for their face value and pay interest at maturity in addition to their face value. Since they are issued with bearer certificates, they must be safeguarded like cash and are generally held for safekeeping at the bank or brokerage firm where they are purchased. Most municipal notes are guaranteed by the full faith and credit of the municipality (its agencies or authorities), but the safest municipal notes are Project notes (minimum cost $25,000) because they are guaranteed by the U.S. government.

Municipal Bonds

Municipal bonds are sold by municipalities to borrow cash for up to forty years for their long-term local projects. Municipal bonds cost a minimum of $1,000, although often the minimum is $5,000. They can originally sell for face value, above face value or below face value and pay interest separately twice a year. They offer the choice of registered or coupon certificates, so they pay interest by coupons or check. Registered municipal securities are difficult to sell before maturity. As a result, they bring lower market resale prices than coupon municipal bonds.

Some municipal bonds are guaranteed by the full faith and credit as well as the taxing power of the municipality—general obligation bonds; other municipal bonds are guaranteed by the revenues from self-supporting projects they finance—revenue bonds (for example, bonds guaranteed by revenues from toll roads whose construction the bonds financed); and still other municipal bonds are guaranteed by a local housing authority as well as by the U.S. government—Public Housing Authority bonds (PHA bonds)—which makes them the safest.

Sometimes municipal bonds have call provisions which allow the municipality to pay them off before they come due, usually at a price above their face value (for more details about call provisions, see page 66).

Buying and Selling Municipal Securities

Municipal governments do not sell securities directly to the investing public. Instead, they sell their securities to groups of banks and brokerage firms (underwriters). Underwriting groups pay for these securities and then assume the risk of reselling them to the public for a profit. Naturally, underwriters insist on paying less for municipal securities that may be harder to resell. Each municipality generally issues new securities in a series which consists of as many as twenty different securities with twenty different maturity dates and paying twenty different yields. Underwriters sell some new municipal securities at face value, others above face value and still others below face value.

You should be careful where you purchase municipal securities because some unscrupulous municipal dealers misrepresent credit ratings and yields. Although municipal dealers are regulated by the Securities and Exchange Commission (SEC), a federal agency established by Congress to protect investors, the Municipal Securities Market was not regulated by the SEC as of 1976. By trading with a reputable, financially sound bank (see page 8) or brokerage firm (see page 71) and by purchasing AAA municipal securities, you eliminate many unnecessary risks.

You can buy and sell municipal securities at banks and brokerage firms. Although you usually pay no commission charge to buy new municipal bonds, you sometimes pay a service charge to buy new municipal notes. Secondhand municipal securities are bought and sold on a net yield basis, which means the banker or broker includes the commission in the price you are quoted. When you buy municipal securities, make sure that they have a legal opinion printed on them or attached to them to indicate they are legally tax-exempt. Secondhand municipal notes and bonds trade like secondhand Treasury notes and bonds (see page 77). The market prices of municipal securities are not listed in city newspapers or financial papers because of the impossibility of listing over 50,000 different municipal securities. If you want their current prices, you can call your banker or broker.

MY CASH Checklist for Municipal Securities
You should buy municipal securities whenever their tax-free yields are more profitable in your tax bracket than taxable yields. Compare securities of similar quality and similar maturity dates ("like" securities) to determine the better buy at that time. The chart on page 154 will be helpful in comparing taxable and tax-free yields in your tax bracket.

Let us review the highlights of the MY CASH checklist for municipal securities. First, select the *Ma*turity date that fits your needs (see page 15). *Y*ields of municipal bonds are affected by their credit ratings—the higher the rating, the lower the yield—as well as by the length of time to maturity—normally, the shorter the time to maturity, the lower the yield. The interest paid by municipal securities is always exempt from federal income tax and sometimes from state and local income taxes as well. Municipal notes are not *C*allable. Municipal bonds should be checked for a call provision; they are usually callable after the first ten or fifteen years at a price above face value. Since you buy municipal bonds for tax-free income, you normally do not *A*nticipate selling them for a profit which is taxable. If you buy municipal securities below face value you will have to pay tax on the discount income you receive at maturity even though the fixed rate of interest you receive is tax-free (for information on discount income, see page 79). The *S*afety of municipal securities is determined by their rating and by their guarantee. Project notes and PHA bonds guaranteed by the U.S. government are the safest. For the safety of municipal securities not guaranteed by the U.S. government, you can use the Moody's and S&P ratings or rely on a MBIA guarantee.

*H*ow much liquidity for municipal securities? They do not offer as much liquidity as "like" Treasury securities or most "like" federal agency securities. The Municipal Securities Market is primarily a buyer's market. You can sell municipal securities at any time, but it is easier to buy them at a reasonable price than it is to sell them for a reasonable price. You can borrow against municipal securities, although generally the Internal Revenue Code does not allow you to deduct the interest you pay. Furthermore, there is a possibility that other interest deductions will not be allowed if you receive the benefit of tax-free interest (consult a tax advisor or telephone your local Internal Revenue Office for more information).

Shirley Wrong Buys Municipal Bonds

Shirley Wrong reads a newspaper ad offering 9% tax-free securities. This sounds like exceptionally good value, so she calls for more information. The nicest man tells her this is a once-in-a-lifetime opportunity. He explains that these bonds are part of a very small new issue but that they are not rated by Moody's or S&P because these advisory services only rate large issues. He assures her they are highest-quality municipal bonds—the small municipality issuing these bonds has always paid its debts. Since the municipality is in her home state, the interest will be

exempt from state and local income taxes as well as
from federal income tax.

Shirley has $5,000 in a passbook savings bank account
that is earning 5% interest or $250 a year. After she
deducts the 30% for taxes she must pay to Uncle Sam,
she keeps only $175, which is reduced even more by
state and local income taxes. On the other hand, $5,000
worth of these municipal bonds will pay $450 annual
income and she can keep all $450.

She buys the municipal bonds and has them registered in her name. One year later, instead of receiving
an interest check, she receives a notice from the municipality stating it is unable to make this interest payment
because its costs have been rising faster than its cash
revenue. Now Shirley is worried about losing her original $5,000 investment as well. She tries to call the bro-
ker who sold her the bonds, but the telephone has been
disconnected. Shirley has bought municipal bonds from
an ad without checking to find out if the municipal
bond dealer is reputable or not—*she is surely wrong.*

P.S. Shirley learns the hard way that ads are for the
benefit of the advertiser and not necessarily to her benefit.

Shirley Wright Buys Municipal Bonds

Shirley Wright reads a newspaper ad offering 9% tax-
free securities. She knows that the Municipal Securities
Market is unregulated and that some unscrupulous
dealers misrepresent the yields and quality of municipal securities. Therefore, instead of calling the firm that
is advertising these securities, which she knows nothing
about, she calls her bank and brokerage firm, both of
which she has already checked and knows are reputable and financially sound. Her banker and broker have
9% tax-free securities for sale, but they inform Shirley
that the reason they pay this exceptionally high yield is

that the securities have a low credit rating, which means there is a greater possibility of default. Shirley realizes these securities are not for her since they do not offer the safety she wants.

Both the banker and the broker feel this is a good time to buy highest-quality AAA municipal securities because their yields are high compared to taxable yields. Shirley compares the tax-free yield offered with the taxable yield in her tax bracket by using the chart on page 154 and decides to invest $10,000 in municipal securities. She prefers PHA bonds guaranteed by the U.S. government.

She uses the MY CASH checklist for municipal securities starting with *M* for *M*aturity date. Because she already has over $25,000 in investments maturing in three years or less, she decides to select a longer maturity date. She has two reasons for this: She wants to lock in the exceptionally high tax-free yield available at this time; and since there is the possibility that Congress may eliminate tax-free securities in the future, she will assure herself of tax-free income for a long time (whether Congress takes this action or not).

She shops for available PHA bonds at her bank and brokerage firm and buys the best value offered to her at that time—$10,000 worth of new Puerto Rico PHA bonds which she buys at face value (par) with a 6½% fixed rate of interest (coupons) maturing in 1995 (not callable before 1990). These bonds are also exempt from state and local income taxes because they were issued by Puerto Rico.

In her 50% tax bracket, the 6½% tax-free yield is equal to a 13% taxable yield, much higher than the 8% yield paid at that time by "like" taxable securities guaranteed by the U.S. government. Although a 6½% tax-free yield is less than the 9% advertised tax-free yield, Shirley feels that protecting her savings is much more

important than receiving 2½% more interest annually
—*she is surely right*.

   The following charts give you detailed information
on municipal notes and municipal bonds.

MUNICIPAL NOTES

Type of Security	IOUs of a municipality, its agencies or authorities— bearer certificates.
Face or Par Values (Minimum)	Usually $25,000 (sometimes $5,000).
Where to Buy, Sell and Redeem	New notes are bought at banks and brokerage firms without a commission charge; secondhand notes are bought and sold on a net yield basis. There is never a redemption charge. These charges can vary and should be checked before an order is placed.
Maturity Dates (New Securities)	Less than 1 year.
Yield (Maximum— 1975) AAA Notes	4.5%. Interest is paid at maturity and is exempt from federal income tax. Also, interest is exempt from state and local income taxes if notes are issued by communities, agencies or

	authorities of the owner's home state, the District of Columbia, Puerto Rico, Guam or the Virgin Islands.
Call Provision	Not callable.
Anticipated Profit or Loss (other than interest income)	The Internal Revenue Code treats gains or losses as interest income which is taxed and considered as ordinary income rather than as a profit or a loss. Therefore, we can only anticipate more or less interest income.
Safety	The repayment of their face value as well as their interest is guaranteed by a municipality or by one of its agencies or authorities.
How Much Liquidity?	Notes can be sold for cash every trading day but do not trade as actively as T-bills or Project notes and therefore bring lower market resale prices than like T-bills or like Project notes.

MUNICIPAL BONDS

Type of Security
: IOUs of a municipality, its agency or authority—coupon or registered certificates.

Face or Par Values (Minimum)
: $1,000 (sometimes $5,000).

Where to Buy, Sell and Redeem
: New bonds are bought at brokerage firms without a commission charge; second-hand bonds bought or sold at brokerage firms usually on a net yield basis. There is never a redemption charge. These charges can vary and should be checked before an order is placed.

Maturity Dates (New Securities)
: Up to 40 years (sometimes longer).

Yield (Maximum— 1975) AAA Bonds
: 6.80%. Interest is paid semiannually and is exempt from federal income tax as well as from state and local income taxes if bonds are issued by communities, agencies or authorities of the owner's home state, the District of Columbia, Puerto Rico, Guam or the Virgin Islands.

*C*all Provision	Usually callable after the first 10 years at a specific price above face value.
*A*nticipated Profit or Loss (other than interest income)	Anticipated profit if the bonds are sold before maturity and yield more than new ones; anticipated loss if the bonds sold yield less than new ones.
*S*afety	The repayment of their face value as well as their interest is guaranteed by a municipality or by one of its agencies or authorities.
*H*ow Much Liquidity?	Bonds can be sold for cash every trading day but do not trade as actively as Treasury securities and therefore bring lower market resale prices than like Treasury securities.

PROJECT NOTES

Type of Security	IOUs of a local public housing authority—bearer certificates.
Face or Par Values (Minimum)	$25,000.
Where to Buy, Sell and Redeem	At commercial banks or brokerage firms for a charge of about $25; there is usually no charge for trades of $100,000 or more. There is never a redemption charge. These charges can vary and should be checked before an order is placed.
Maturity Dates (New Securities)	Less than 1 year—local authorities sell new project notes on the 2nd and 3rd Tuesday of every month (in 1975).
Yield (Maximum— 1975)	4.5%. Interest is paid at maturity and is exempt from federal income tax as well as from state and local income taxes if notes are issued by public housing authorities of the owner's home state, the District of Columbia, Puerto Rico, Guam or the Virgin Islands.

Call Provision	Not callable.
Anticipated Profit or Loss (other than interest income)	The Internal Revenue Code treats gains or losses as interest income which is taxed and considered as ordinary income rather than as a profit or a loss. Therefore, we can only anticipate more or less interest income.
Safety	The repayment of their face value as well as their interest is guaranteed by a local housing authority and indirectly guaranteed by the U.S. government.
How Much Liquidity?	Notes can be sold for cash every trading day but do not trade actively as T-bills. As a result, their market resale prices are lower than those of like T-bills.

PUBLIC HOUSING AUTHORITY BONDS
(PHA BONDS)

Type of Security

IOUs of a local public housing authority—coupon or registered certificates.

Face or Par Values (Minimum)

$1,000 (sometimes $5,000).

Where to Buy, Sell and Redeem

New bonds are bought at brokerage firms without a commission charge; secondhand bonds bought or sold at brokerage firms on a net yield basis. There is never a redemption charge. These charges can vary and should be checked before an order is placed.

Maturity Dates (New Securities)

Up to 40 years (sometimes longer).

Yield (Maximum—1975)

6.80%. Interest paid semiannually and is exempt from federal income tax. Also, interest is exempt from state and local income taxes if notes are issued by public housing authorities of the owner's home state; the District of Columbia; Puerto Rico; Guam or the Virgin Islands.

*C*all Provision	Usually callable after the first 15 years at a specific price above face value.
*A*nticipated Profit or Loss (other than interest income)	Anticipated profit if the bonds are sold before maturity and yield more than new ones; anticipated loss if the bonds sold yield less than new ones.
*S*afety	The repayment of their face value as well as their interest is guaranteed by a local housing authority and indirectly guaranteed by the U.S. government.
*H*ow Much Liquidity?	Bonds can be sold for cash every trading day but do not trade as actively as Treasury securities. As a result, their market resale prices are lower than those of like Treasury securities.

6

Should You Loan Your Money
to a Corporation by Purchasing Corporate Bonds?
or
Should You Be a Part Owner of a Corporation by Purchasing Corporate Stock?

Corporations raise money to operate and expand their companies by borrowing money (selling bonds) or by taking in new partners (selling stocks). When corporations sell bonds they promise to pay bondholders a fixed annual rate of interest and to repay the face value of their bonds when they come due. Bondholders know in advance what their annual income will be and how much they will be repaid at maturity.

When corporations sell stocks, they promise stockholders (partners) the opportunity to share in corporate profits. Stockholders receive an annual income (dividends) only if corporations make a profit, and they get cash for the value of the stocks themselves by selling them to other speculators in the stock market. The market price for a stock will usually increase or decrease in relation to how much or how little a corporation earns. Stockholders are never sure of what their annual income will be or how much their stock will be worth in the future.

When you buy bonds, you are loaning your money to a corporation which pays you a fixed annual income and repays your original investment, whereas when you buy stocks you are one of the owners of a corporation which offers you the possibility of making large profits if the company is successful or of losing part or all of your original investment if the company is not successful. Not everyone should be the owner of a business, in this case, a stockholder. The decision to buy stock depends upon your financial condition and your emotional make-up. If the decline of stock prices could lower your standard of living or cause you great anxiety, you should invest in corporate bonds and stay out of the stock market.

CORPORATE BONDS

When you buy corporate bonds you are loaning a minimum of $1,000 to a corporation for a period of days to over thirty years. The corporation pays you a fixed rate of annual interest and repays the face value (par) of

172   DOLLARS AND ENE

your bonds on the date they come due. Although a
corporation usually does not repay its bonds before maturity (unless there is a call provision, see page 66), you
can get cash before maturity by borrowing against
bonds at a bank or by selling bonds in the Corporate
Bond Market as you would sell secondhand Treasury
securities in the Government Securities Market (see
page 77). However, secondhand corporate bonds usually bring lower market resale prices than "like" Treasury securities because they do not trade as actively.

Since corporate bonds are neither federally insured
nor guaranteed by the U.S. government, they are not
considered as safe as Treasury securities or agency
securities. To compensate for this additional risk, corporate bonds generally pay higher yields than Treasury
or agency securities.

Although all corporations intend to repay the face
value of their bonds when they come due, not all corporations are able to repay bondholders at maturity and
therefore must default. If a corporation goes into bankruptcy, bondholders, as well as other creditors, have
first claim on the cash the corporation receives from the
sale of its remaining assets. In other words, whatever
cash is available must be used to repay creditors before
stockholders (owners) receive any cash.

When you buy corporate bonds, you want bonds
more likely to be repaid under all circumstances. Unless you are able to analyze corporate financial statements, you usually must rely on the ratings of independent advisory services such as Moody Investor Service
and Standard & Poor to determine the safety (quality)
of corporate bonds. These ratings go from highest quality AAA to a very risky lowest quality (see page 153). A
broker (and sometimes the investment department of
a bank) will give you corporate bond ratings over the
telephone.

When you purchase a corporation's bonds, you are

loaning money to the corporation. Corporate bonds are referred to by different names which identify different maturity dates. They are called commercial paper and bankers' acceptances when they originally come due in one year or less, corporate notes when they originally come due in one to fifteen years and corporate bonds when they originally come due in up to twenty-five years.

Short-Term Commercial Paper and Bankers' Acceptances

Commercial paper ($25,000 minimum face value) and bankers' acceptances ($10,000 or sometimes $25,000 minimum face value) originally come due in one year or less. They are the corporate version of T-bills and are bought for the same reasons (see page 64). Like T-bills, commercial paper and bankers' acceptances are issued with bearer certificates and pay interest by selling for less than their face value. They can be bought and sold at banks and brokerage firms which charge a service fee of about $25 for trades of less than $100,000 and generally do not charge for trades of $100,000 or more.

Commercial paper, which is issued by all types of major corporations (financial, industrial, transportation and utility), is rated by Dun & Bradstreet advisory service (prime 1 stands for highest quality). Bankers' acceptances, which are issued by major banks, are not rated by an advisory service. You can use the ratings given to major banks on their long-term securities (which are rated) in order to judge the quality of their shorter-term bankers' acceptances.

Highest-quality commercial paper and bankers' acceptances are attractive investments because of their higher yields. In 1975, for example, they yielded up to 9.25% when T-bills were yielding a maximum of 7.28%.

Corporate Notes and Bonds

Corporations sell conventional corporate notes and bonds (minimum $1,000) which originally come due in one to twenty-five years. They are the corporate version of Treasury notes and bonds and are bought for the same reasons (see page 66). Like new Treasury notes and bonds, new corporate notes and bonds originally sell for their $1,000 face value, pay interest separately twice a year and offer the choice of coupon or registered certificates. Unlike Treasury notes and bonds, they can be sold with registered certificates immediately and without penalty.

In the mid-1970s, corporate bonds issued by electric utility companies were yielding more than other "like" corporate bonds. Why? Because investors believed electric utility companies were in a profit squeeze— their fuel costs and new equipment costs were rising and, at the same time, utility users were fighting increases in utility rates. Since this could affect the future ability of these corporations to pay interest or to repay the face value of their bonds, investors insisted on higher yields.

What has also made highest-quality AAA corporate notes and bonds attractive investments is their high yields. In 1975, for example, they yielded up to 9.7% when Treasury notes and bonds were yielding a maximum of 8.5%.

Several dozen corporations also sell unconventional notes and bonds, such as floating rate notes and convertible bonds. Floating rate notes originally sell for their $1,000 face value (sometimes a $5,000 minimum), originally come due in up to fifteen years and pay interest every six months.

What makes floating rate notes unconventional is that their rate of interest is not fixed but "floats" (goes up and down) with the current rate of interest paid by three-month T-bills. For the first six to nine months, floating rate notes pay the same rate of interest as other "like" conventional corporate notes (up to 10% in 1974). After that, they generally pay 1% to 1½% more annually than the current annual rate of interest paid by three-month T-bills. After the first few years, at your request, corporations will repay the face value of floating rate notes on every interest-payment date.

Their floating rate of interest gives investors a hedge against rising interest rates and yet, after the first few years, if interest rates decline, investors can get cash for their full face value every six months (on any interest-payment day). Whenever short-term interest rates are rising, floating rate notes can be profitable investments. Chase Manhattan Bank, Citicorp and Standard Oil of Indiana are a few corporations that have sold floating rate notes.

Convertible bonds are long-term corporate bonds that originally sell for their face value (minimum $1,000). The corporation pays a fixed rate of annual interest semiannually until convertible bonds come due (up to twenty-five years) and repays their face value at maturity.

What makes these bonds unconventional is that, during their lifetime, they are "convertible" into a specific number of shares of the same corporation's common stock. This convertible feature allows investors to profit from a rise in the price of the company's common stock. If the price of the common stock rises, the price of a convertible bond also rises because there is more value to the shares which the bond can be exchanged for.

Investors like to buy convertible bonds because they can make large profits if the price of the corporation's common stock rises, and yet if the price of the stock declines, their losses are limited because a convertible bond is always worth its face value at maturity. Corporations like to sell convertible bonds because they can

pay a lower fixed rate of interest than they can pay on
"like" conventional bonds. Why? Investors are willing
to accept a lower fixed rate of interest in exchange for
their convertible feature.

Past experience indicates that corporations usually
issue convertible bonds when investors are optimistic
and when the price of their common stock is relatively
high. This is not a profitable time for investors to buy
convertible bonds. In general, it is more profitable to
buy secondhand convertible bonds of corporations
whose stock you want to own in the future when the
bonds sell below face value because the price of their
common stock is relatively low.

You can get a list of convertible bonds from your
broker. Occidental Petroleum, Armstrong Rubber and
W. R. Grace & Co. are a few corporations which have
issued convertible bonds.

Buying and Selling Corporate Bonds
The Securities and Exchange Commission (SEC) regulates corporate bond dealers and the Corporate Bond
Market. Before corporations are allowed to sell new
notes or new long-term bonds, they are usually required to file a report with the SEC as well as with state
authorities called a Prospectus. A Prospectus is a long
report that describes in detail the securities as well as
the business of the corporation selling them and gives
information that may not otherwise be available to you.
In the past, the Prospectus has been written in technical language which is difficult to understand; however,
in 1975, the SEC proposed the use of a short-form Prospectus which will be easier to read. Before you buy new
bond issues get the Prospectus from your broker and
find out how the company plans to use the money from
the sale of these securities, the company's recent developments and if any lawsuits are pending against the
company.

Instead of selling new bonds directly to the investing public, corporations sell them to groups of brokerage firms and security dealers called underwriters, who then resell them to the investing public for a profit. Underwriters advertise new bond offerings in the financial section of many city newspapers and in the *Wall Street Journal.* For example, you may have read on July 15, 1974:

$250,000,000
FORD MOTOR COMPANY
9¼% Debentures due July 15, 1994
Price 100%
Securities are redeemable prior to maturity
Upon request, a copy of the Prospectus
may be obtained from any underwriter
who may legally distribute it within such state.

The names of over sixty underwriting firms were also listed in this ad, which announced the sale of $250 million worth of new Ford Motor Company debentures (bonds guaranteed by the credit of the company). These bonds pay a 9¼% fixed rate of interest every year until they come due on July 15, 1994. If you had bought bonds that day, they would have cost 100% of their face value. "Securities are redeemable prior to maturity" means the Ford Motor Company can call these bonds before they come due. Any of the underwriters would give you a Prospectus as well as any other information about the bonds you wanted to know, such as their minimum face value ($1,000), their rating (AAA —highest quality) and the details of their call provision (callable after the first ten years at a price above face value). Since these were new bonds, there was no commission charge. Your total cost for each bond would be $1,000 (its face value).

After these new bonds were sold, they began trading as secondhand bonds in the Corporate Bond Market just like secondhand Treasury bonds trade in the Government Securities Market (see page 77). The market prices of secondhand corporate bonds (particularly those sold on major exchanges) are listed daily in city newspapers and in the *Wall Street Journal* along with their current yield.

The current yield is the percentage of the fixed rate of annual interest a bond pays in relation to its market price (figured by dividing the fixed rate of interest by the market price). If the market price of a bond is the same as its face value (say, $1,000), then the current yield is always its fixed rate of interest. If the market price of a bond is less than its face value (say $900), then the current yield is more than its fixed rate of interest. And if the market price of a bond is more than its face value (say $1,100), then the current yield is less than its fixed rate of interest. However, if the market price of a bond is more or less than its $1,000 face value, the current yield is not the total yield you receive. Why? Because the current yield must be increased by the discount income paid at maturity or decreased by premiums not repaid at maturity which is the yield to maturity. Therefore, if you are buying bonds below or above face value, ask your banker or broker for the yield to maturity (they have prefigured tables).

MY CASH Checklist for Corporate Bonds
Let us review corporate bonds by using the MY CASH checklist. The *M*aturity dates of corporate bonds range from days to over thirty years, which can fit your varying needs (see page 15). Their *Y*ields are affected by their credit ratings (the higher their rating, the less the element of risk and therefore the lower their yield) and also by their maturity dates (normally the shorter time to maturity, the lower their yield). Commercial paper, bankers' acceptances and most corporate notes are not *C*allable, whereas long-term corporate bonds are gen-

erally callable after the first five or ten years at a price above face value. You can Anticipate a profit if you sell corporate notes or long-term corporate bonds that yield more than like new ones, and you can anticipate a loss if they yield less than like new ones. The Safety of all corporate bonds depends on the financial condition of the corporation that guarantees them. Normally, the higher the bonds' credit rating, the safer they are. How much liquidity for corporate notes and bonds? There is not as much as for Treasury securities, although corporate bonds listed on the New York Stock Exchange trade actively and usually bring relatively higher market resale prices than other like corporate bonds.

Shirley Wright Buys Corporate Bonds and Treasury Securities

Shirley Wright sold her resort condominium and has $20,000 in cash to invest. She wants to compare corporate securities with agency and Treasury securities to determine the best buy.

She decides to stagger her maturity dates so that she has money coming due which can be reinvested every year. Since she already owns Treasury notes coming due in two years and agency securities coming due in three years, she decides to invest half of her $20,000 in securities maturing in one year and the other half in securities maturing in four or five years. In this way she will have about $10,000 coming due almost every year for the next four or five years. In addition, she owns $10,000 worth of municipal bonds coming due in twenty years.

She calls her banker and asks for the best yields on Treasury securities, agency securities and AAA corporate bonds maturing in one year as well as those maturing in five years. After using the MY CASH checklist to compare what is offered, she decides to buy $10,000

worth of AAA Sears Roebuck bonds maturing in one
year and yielding 8⅛% rather than buying Treasury
securities yielding 6⅛% or agency securities yielding
6¼%. She gives up the maximum safety of a U.S. government guarantee to receive $200 more income a
year from AAA Sears bonds which she believes are safe
and will be repaid at maturity.

Shirley decides to invest the other $10,000 in five-
year Treasury notes yielding 8⅜% because like agency
securities were yielding 8½% and like corporate bonds
were yielding 8¾%. She is not willing to give up the
maximum safety of a U.S. government guarantee and
the maximum liquidity offered by Treasury notes for
the small difference in these yields.

She is comfortable with her purchases. She has inflation protection if interest rates rise because she can
reinvest the money coming due every year at higher
interest rates. If interest rates decline, however, she
will receive the currently high interest rates for five
years from Treasury notes and for twenty years from
municipal bonds—*she is surely right.*

The following individual accounts of bankers' acceptances, commercial paper, conventional corporate notes
and bonds, floating rate notes and convertible bonds
will be helpful if you want to buy these securities or if
you want to compare them with other securities.

BANKERS' ACCEPTANCES

Type of Security

IOUs guaranteed by a commercial bank—bearer certificates.

Face or Par Values (minimum)

$25,000 (sometimes less).

Where to Buy, Sell and Redeem

Usually at commercial banks for a charge of $25; there is usually no charge for trades of $100,000 or more. There is never a redemption charge. These charges can vary and should be checked before an order is placed.

Maturity Date (New Securities)

30, 60, 90 and 180 days.

Yield (Maximum— 1975)

8.5%. Interest is paid by selling for less than face value.

Call Provision

Not callable.

Anticipated Profit or Loss (other than interest income)

There can be no anticipated profit or loss because the difference between their purchase price and redemption price (or sale price) is interest. Furthermore, the Internal Revenue Code states that this income is taxed as ordinary interest income, not as a profit or a loss.

| Safety | The repayment of their face value as well as their interest is guaranteed by the bank. |
| How Much Liquidity? | Bankers' acceptances can be sold for cash every trading day but do not trade as actively as T-bills. As a result, their market resale prices are lower than those of like T-bills. |

COMMERCIAL PAPER

Type of Security — IOUs of a corporation—coupon certificates.

Face or Par Values (minimum) — $25,000.

Where to Buy, Sell and Redeem — At commercial banks or brokerage firms for a charge of $25; there is usually no charge for trades of $100,000 or more. There is never a redemption charge. These charges can vary and should be checked before an order is placed.

Maturity Date (New Securities) — Days to 270 days.

Yield (Maximum—1975) — 9.25%. Interest is paid by selling for less than face value.

Call Provision — Not callable.

Anticipated Profit or Loss (other than interest income) — There can be no anticipated profit or loss because the difference between their purchase price and redemption price (or sale price) is interest. Furthermore, the Internal Revenue Code states that this income is taxed as ordinary interest income, not as a profit or a loss.

| Safety | The repayment of their face value as well as their interest is guaranteed by a commercial bank. |
| How Much Liquidity? | Commercial paper can be sold for cash every trading day but does not trade as actively as T-bills. As a result, market resale prices are lower than those of like T-bills. |

CONVENTIONAL CORPORATE NOTES AND BONDS

Type of Security	IOUs of a corporation— coupon or registered certificates.
Face or Par Values (Minimum)	$1,000.
Where to Buy, Sell and Redeem	At brokerage firms with usually no commission charge for buying new notes and bonds; secondhand notes and bonds are traded on a net yield basis. There is never a redemption charge. These charges can vary and should be checked before an order is placed.
Maturity Dates (New Securities)	Notes usually up to 10 years; bonds up to 30 years and sometimes longer.
Yield (Maximum— 1975) AAA	9.5%. Interest is paid semiannually.
Call Provision	Notes are usually not callable; bonds are usually callable.
Anticipated Profit or Loss (other than interest income)	Anticipated profit if the notes or bonds are sold before maturity and yield more than new ones; anticipated loss if the notes and bonds are sold when they yield less than new ones.

*S*afety	The repayment of their face value as well as their interest is guaranteed by the credit or by specific assets of a corporation.
*H*ow Much Liquidity?	Corporate bonds can be sold for cash every trading day, but do not trade as actively as Treasury securities. As a result, they bring lower market resale prices than do like Treasury securities. But AAA corporate notes and bonds listed on major exchanges when part of a large original issue of $50 million or more trade the most actively and are therefore the most liquid corporate notes or bonds.

FLOATING RATE NOTES

Type of Security	IOUs of a corporation—bearer certificates.
Face or Par Values (Minimum)	$5,000 (sometimes $1,000).
Where to Buy, Sell and Redeem	At brokerage firms with usually no commission charge for buying new notes; secondhand notes trade on a net yield basis. There is never a redemption charge. These charges can vary and should be checked before an order is placed.
Maturity Dates (New Securities)	Up to 15 years but usually redeemable after the first 2 years on any interest-payment date.
Yield (Maximum—1975)	9.7%.* Interest is paid semiannually and is linked to the rate of 3-month T-bills—usually 1% to 1½% higher. However, the first several months they yield the going market interest rate for like corporate notes.
Call Provision	Not callable.

Anticipated Profit or Loss (other than interest income)	Anticipated profit if the notes are sold before maturity and yield more than other like notes at that time; anticipated loss if the notes are sold when they yield less than other like notes at that time.
Safety	The repayment of their face value as well as their interest is guaranteed by the credit of the corporation.
How Much Liquidity?	Floating rate notes can be sold for cash every trading day but do not trade as actively as standard corporate bonds. As a result, they bring lower market resale prices than do like corporate notes. However, they are redeemable every 6 months on interest-payment date and so offer more liquidity than other corporate notes.

*Floating rate notes: Standard Oil of Indiana due 1989 used as example.

CONVERTIBLE BONDS

Type of Security	IOUs of a corporation that can be "converted" into a specific number of shares of the corporation's common stock at a specific price— coupon and registered certificates.
Face or Par Values (Minimum)	$1,000 (sometimes $5,000).
Where to Buy, Sell and Redeem	At brokerage firms with usually no commission charge for buying new bonds; secondhand bonds trade on a net yield basis. There is never a redemption charge. These charges can vary and should be checked before an order is placed.
Maturity Dates (New Securities)	Up to 25 years.
Yield (Maximum— 1975)	10.59%.* Interest is paid semiannually.
Call Provision	Sometimes callable.

Anticipated Profit or Loss (other than interest income)	Anticipated profit if the bonds are sold before maturity and yield more than new ones or if the price of the common stock is higher than when the bonds were purchased; anticipated loss if the bonds sold yield less than new ones or the price of the stock is lower than when the bonds were purchased.
Safety	The repayment of their face value as well as their interest is guaranteed by the credit of the corporation.
How Much Liquidity?	Convertible bonds can be sold for cash every trading day but do not trade as actively as standard corporate bonds. As a result, they bring lower market resale prices than do like corporate bonds.

*McGraw-Hill 3⅞% convertible bonds due May 1992 used as an example.

CORPORATE STOCKS

When you buy corporate stock, you are buying part of a corporation and you become a part owner. The corporation gives you a certificate registered in your name which is your receipt of ownership. Most corporations distribute profit (dividends) to stockholders (part owners) four times a year. The more profit corporations earn, the more dividend income they generally distribute. If they do not earn a profit, they have no money to distribute as dividends.

If you want the money for your stock, you can borrow at a bank by putting up your stock certificate as collateral or you can sell stock to other speculators in the stock market. The market price you receive for a stock changes constantly, so you may receive more or less than your original cost. Stock prices are affected by developments within the corporation itself, by international, economic and political developments as well as by changes in interest rates.

There are two kinds of stock—the kind you "commonly" think of as stock, or common stock, and the kind that receives certain "preferential" treatment, or preferred stock.

Common Stocks

The one question all speculators want answered is: Which common stocks will be the profitable ones? Dozens of different systems have been suggested for selecting profitable stocks, such as buying stocks of corporations in certain industries; buying stocks that are leaders in their industries; buying stocks that sell below their book value (the amount of assets the corporation owns for each share of stock outstanding); or buying stocks that sell for less than ten times their annual earnings. You should remember, however, that there is no sure system.

The ideal stock would be one paying large dividends and offering great growth potential, but such a stock rarely exists. A stock that pays a large dividend income usually does not offer above average growth potential, and a growth stock usually does not pay a large dividend income.

If you buy stocks primarily for income, select the stocks of corporations that have a long history of profitable operations because corporations distribute dividends from earned profits. According to a study made by the New York Stock Exchange in the 1960s, the majority of corporations whose stocks were listed on the Exchange distributed one-half of their annual profits to stockholders.

Before you buy stocks for income, compare their yields with bond yields. For example, in 1945, it was worth risking money to buy stocks for income because bonds were yielding only 3% and stocks were yielding much more. On the other hand, in 1974, there was no reason to risk money to buy stocks for income because highest-quality bonds were yielding up to 12% annually, much more than high-quality stocks were yielding.

If you buy stocks primarily for growth, select the stocks of corporations whose earnings are constantly increasing and that have prospects for continued growth in the future. Past experience indicates that the stocks of corporations whose earnings increase consistently are the ones most likely to rise in market price. Should the price of a stock you own increase by $10, $5 or even $2 a share, you can then make a profit by selling it.

During periods of rapid economic growth like the 1950s and 1960s, growth stocks doubled and tripled in price every five to ten years. These figures are misleading, however, because in order to determine the average growth you can expect from stocks, you must combine the bad years with the good years. The University of Chicago conducted a study for the forty-year period from 1926 to 1965 for all the stocks listed on the New York Stock Exchange and determined their annual average return (including dividends, the reinvestment of dividends and the increase in price) was 9.3%.

You can get an idea as to a corporation's earnings, its dividend stability, its ability to withstand business reversals, its ability to get financing and its management from its stock rating. Common-stock ratings given by Moody's and S&P are based on the present and past performances of a corporation and range from A+ (highest quality) to A (high quality) to A— (above quality) all the way to D, which stands for stocks of companies that are reorganizing to avoid bankruptcy. But selecting stocks usually requires projections into the future of a corporation. The future earnings of a corporation depend upon considerations such as new competition, new government regulations, the future trend of business and future profit margins.

When you try to predict the tomorrow's earnings of a corporation today you can only make a "guestimate." The better your information, the better your chance for making a good "guestimate." If you decide to buy common stocks, take the time and effort to get all the information from the research department of your brokerage firm. In addition, ask your broker for the current individual stock write-up published by Standard & Poor. That way, you can make judgments on facts rather than on tips or rumors. Still, no matter how good your information is, you may still pick losers. One way to protect yourself is to spread your risk by speculating in a few common stocks rather than buying only one stock.

After you have purchased common stocks, continue to watch for developments that may affect the earnings or growth of that corporation; for example, read the quarterly and annual reports mailed to you by the corporation. Although most investors try to select a good time to buy stocks, they are rarely as careful about selecting a good time to sell stocks. It is usually a good time to sell a stock when you can improve your investment position elsewhere.

Preferred Stocks

Corporations pay a fixed dividend on their preferred stocks which is usually higher than the dividend they pay on their common stocks. Preferred-stock dividends are fixed by the corporation when the stocks are originally issued and are stated on their stock certificates, whereas common stock dividends vary from year to year. Although the fixed dividends paid by preferred stocks can be reduced or omitted, corporations must always pay preferred-stock dividends before they can pay common-stock dividends. And, in case of bankruptcy, preferred stockholders have claim on the corporation's assets before common stockholders.

In exchange for these "preferred" rights, preferred stockholders generally do not share in a corporation's profit beyond the fixed dividends they receive. As a result, preferred stocks are bought for their yields, that is, their fixed dividend income. In actuality, this makes preferred stocks more like corporate bonds than like common stocks since their market prices go up and down primarily with interest rates rather than with the earnings of the corporation. Preferred stocks, like corporate bonds, usually have call provisions which allow the corporation to redeem them for a specific price after the first five or ten years. In addition, preferred stocks are rated by Moody's and S&P like corporate bonds, not like common stocks. The S&P and Moody's ratings go, respectively, from AAA or Aaa (highest quality) to AA or Aa (high quality) to A (above average quality) all the way to C, which stands for preferred stock that no longer pay dividends.

Sometimes corporations issue preferred stock with bonuses called convertible preferred stocks or cumulative preferred stocks. The bonuses which convertible preferred stocks and cumulative preferred stocks offer attract more investors. This enables corporations to pay relatively lower fixed dividends.

Convertible preferred stocks allow the stockholders to "convert" their stock into a specific number of shares of the common stock of the same corporation (similar to convertible bonds, see page 174). Cumulative preferred stocks offer stockholders a guarantee that any fixed dividend payments that are omitted will "accumulate" from one year to the next and that all these omitted fixed dividends will be paid to preferred stockholders before any dividends can be paid to common stockholders.

Although highest-quality preferred stocks can be attractive speculations for investors when they yield at least 1% more than the long-term bonds of the same corporation, they are bought most frequently by corporations. Why? Because when a corporation receives dividend income from another corporation, it is 85% exempt from federal income tax. Corporations, therefore, buy preferred stocks for their fixed dividend income in order to take advantage of this tax benefit.

Stockholders' Responsibilities and Rights
Most stockholders spend their time watching the market prices of their stock instead of watching the company's progress. Stockholders should read the quarterly and annual reports of that corporation to determine whether management is doing a good job.

Stockholders have one vote for each share of stock they own. They are entitled to vote for the directors of a corporation and sometimes they vote on other company business. Stockholders can vote in person (by attending company meetings) or by mail (by proxy).

Corporations sometimes raise money by offering certain privileges, called rights, to their stockholders. These rights give stockholders the opportunity to buy securities directly from the corporation for a very short period of time at a price below the current market price. For example, AT&T offered stockholders the "right" to buy one additional share of stock for each twenty shares they owned at a price of $100 a share when the market price of AT&T stock was $146. Stockholders generally have the choice of buying the additional shares of stock at this favorable price or of selling their rights to other investors. When you receive rights to buy securities either exercise them or sell them immediately because they are usually valuable for only a short period of time.

Stock Exchanges and the Over-the-Counter Market
Stocks of the largest and most profitable companies usually trade on the New York Stock Exchange or on the American Stock Exchange. Regional exchanges such as the Midwest Stock Exchange and the Pacific Coast Stock Exchange originally traded stocks of local companies, although in recent years they largely trade stocks also listed on the New York Stock Exchange. A stock exchange is located in one building, and it is on the floor of that exchange that the orders from investors who want to buy or sell stock are matched and executed.

Stocks of banks and insurance companies as well as the stocks of a few industrial giants trade in the over-the-counter market; however, most over-the-counter stocks are generally those of smaller companies. As these smaller companies grow and prosper, they usually apply for listing on a major stock exchange.

The over-the-counter market is not located in one

place. Instead, it is a network made up of a communication system and computers which give dealers the bid and asked prices of the over-the-counter securities. The buy and sell orders for over-the-counter stocks are negotiated with many different security dealers located throughout the country who keep inventories of these stocks. So, do not hesitate to ask your broker to shop for a better price if you want to buy or sell stocks traded in the over-the-counter market.

Buying and Selling Stocks

The stock market and brokerage firms are regulated by the SEC. Before a corporation can sell a new issue of stock, it is usually required to file a Prospectus with the SEC (see page 176). Corporations sell new issues of stock for less than the asking price to groups of brokerage firms and security dealers, called underwriters, who then make a profit by reselling the new issues to the investing public at the asking price. That is why you are not charged a commission when you buy new stock offerings. You are, however, charged a commission when you buy secondhand stocks. But since these charges are not fixed, it is possible to negotiate the commission you pay, particularly if you buy in large dollar amounts (over $50,000). Also, if you deal with brokerage firms that have eliminated research departments, you generally pay lower commission rates.

The market prices of many stocks sold on major exchanges and in the over-the-counter market are published every trading day in the *Wall Street Journal* and on the financial page of many city newspapers. The market price of a share of stock is quoted in dollars with fractions of ⅛. For example, a price of 28⅜ means $28.37½ per share or $2,837.50 for a hundred shares of stock. You can also call a broker to get the current market price as well as the current dividend of any stock that interests you. Be sure to

deal with a reputable and financially sound brokerage firm (see page 71).

Dow Jones Industrial Averages

You hear about the Dow Jones averages constantly.
There are actually several Dow Jones averages, but the
most popular is the Dow Jones Industrial average (DJI).
The DJI is a compilation based on the market prices of
thirty well-known common stocks (such as General Mo-
tors, AT&T, Sears Roebuck) that trade on the New York
Stock Exchange. The DJI indicates the general movement of stock prices. When you hear, "DJI up 2," that
indicates the trend of stock prices is higher today than
yesterday, and when you hear, "Dow dips 4," that indicates the trend of stock prices is lower today than yesterday. The larger the number of points the DJI goes up
or down, the more stock prices are moving up or down.
In the past, the movement of the DJI has been used by
professionals to predict many major turning points in
the economy. Some professionals today, however, think
the 30 DJI average is no longer representative and
prefer to use the Standard & Poor 500 Index (listed
daily) because this index is made up of 86% of all the
stocks traded on the New York Stock Exchange.

Buying on Margin

Up to now, we have discussed buying securities for
100% cash and keeping your own certificates, which is
generally the best way for the average investor to buy
securities. However, you can also buy securities on margin. This means you put up only part of the money
required to buy the securities and you borrow the balance from the brokerage firm. The brokerage firm
charges interest on the amount of money you borrow
and also keeps the certificates of the securities as collateral for the loan in the name of the brokerage firm, not
in your name.

The Federal Reserve Board determines the amount of cash you are allowed to borrow to buy on margin. In recent years, you could borrow as much as 50% to buy stock on margin and as much as 95% to buy bonds on margin.

Let's assume you have $1,250 to speculate and you want to buy stock that cost $25 a share at a time when you are allowed to borrow 50% to buy on margin. You can either buy fifty shares of a stock and pay $1,250 cash or you can buy a hundred shares of the same stock on margin and pay $1,250 in cash and borrow the other $1,250 from your broker. If the price of this stock rises, you would make twice as much money had you borrowed to buy a hundred shares on margin than you would had you bought fifty shares for cash, whereas if the price of the stock declines you would lose twice as much money had you borrowed to buy a hundred shares of stock on margin than you would had you bought only fifty shares for cash.

Furthermore, you are required to keep cash in your margin account equal to 25% or more of the current market value of the stock. As a result, whenever the price of a stock bought on margin declines to the point where you no longer have at least 25% of its value in your margin account, your broker will ask you to deposit more cash since the brokerage firm does not want to take a chance on losing the money you borrowed to buy that stock. If you do not deposit more cash (or collateral) immediately, your broker will sell the securities in your margin account and first take the cash proceeds to repay the money you borrowed from the brokerage firm and then return to you any cash that is left.

Margin buying is used primarily by professionals who want the leverage of making $50,000 do the work of $100,000, but it is generally not recommended for the average investor. Why? Because by the time you pay the interest and commission charges to the brokerage firm for an average transaction, the amount of profit you make if the price of the stock rises does not justify the risk of losing a large part or all of your money if the price of the stock declines.

Short Selling

You normally buy stock when you believe the price of a stock will rise. If your judgment proves right, you make a profit by subsequently selling that stock for more than you paid. On the other hand, if your judgment proves wrong, you take a loss by subsequently selling that stock for less than you paid.

You can also make money in the stock market by short selling when you believe the price of a stock will decline. Short selling reverses the normal procedure. First, you temporarily borrow the stock from the brokerage firm. Then, you sell that stock that you do not own. Should your judgment prove right, you make a profit by subsequently buying back that stock for less than you originally sold it for. Should your judgment prove wrong, however, you take a loss by subsequently buying back that stock for more than you originally sold it for. You replace the stock you borrowed from the brokerage firm when you repurchase the stock.

Short selling is always done on margin. When you originally sell stock you do not own (that is, stock you borrowed from the broker), you are required to put up the same amount of cash (or collateral) that the Federal Reserve Board requires if you were buying stock on margin. Furthermore, you must maintain in your margin account at least 25% of the cash value of the stock you sold. In case the price of the stock rises to the point where you have less than 25% in your margin account, your broker will ask for additional cash (or collateral). If you do not come up with more money immediately, the broker will buy back the stock you sold to replace the stock you borrowed, and if there is any cash left it is returned to you.

Short selling is risky and best left to professionals. Although gains from short selling are limited, losses are not. If you sell a stock short, the most that stock can go down is 100%. For example, the maximum profit you can make by selling short a stock that has the price of $20 a share is $20 a share. On the other hand, the price of a $20 stock can rise 100% to $40 a share, 200% to $60 a share or even 300% to $80 a share, and so there is no limit to the price you must pay when you subsequently buy back the stock.

Another type of short selling is selling against the box, or short selling stock you own (not borrowed stock). This is done for tax purposes. Federal tax regulations allow you to use selling short against the box to postpone a profit on stock until the next year. Federal tax regulations, however, do not allow you to use short selling against the box to convert a short-term gain (under six months) into a long-term gain (capital gain).

When you sell short against the box, you are neutralizing your position because you own the stock. You do not make a profit if the price of the stock goes up and you do not take a loss if the price of the stock goes down. In other words, your gains and losses cancel each other. The only cost for short selling against the box is the commission you pay the brokerage firm.

MY CASH Checklist for Corporate Stocks
There is more risk in buying high-quality corporate stocks than in buying high-quality corporate bonds. But when interest rates are low and prospects for corporate growth look promising, stocks are usually more profitable. Let's use the MY CASH checklist to go over the highlights of corporate stocks.

Stocks do not have *M*aturity dates because corporations do not promise to repay the par value of stocks on any date in the future. The *Y*ields paid by stocks are unpredictable because corporations only pay dividends

when they have the ability to do so. Since the first $100
you receive in dividend income can be excluded from
your federal income tax, you should try to receive $100
tax-free dividend income annually (from either common or preferred stocks). Common stocks do not have
a *C*all provision; however, preferred stocks are usually
callable at specific prices. You can normally *A*nticipate
a profit if you sell common stocks of corporations whose
earnings are increasing at a time when buyers are optimistic. If you make a profit from the sale of stock held
longer than six months, this profit is usually taxed at
one-half the ordinary income tax rate (the capital gains
rate). You can generally anticipate a loss if you sell common stocks of corporations whose earnings are declin-
ing. Also, you can anticipate a profit if you sell preferred
stocks that yield more than new preferred stocks and
you can anticipate a loss if they yield less than new
preferred stocks. The *S*afety of a stock depends on the
future earning ability as well as the cash position of the
issuing corporation. Furthermore, the preferred stocks
of corporations offer more safety than the common
stocks of the same corporations. *H*ow much liquidity
for corporate stocks? Although you can normally sell
stocks for cash at any time, stocks of large, well-established companies that trade on major exchanges in
large volume offer more liquidity because they usually
bring relatively better market prices.

Shirley Wrong Buys Stocks

On a flight home from a vacation trip, Shirley Wrong
sits next to a very friendly business executive. They
chat all the way, which makes her trip most enjoyable.
She is particularly grateful for the confidential information he shares with her about the corporation he works
for. The executive tells her that this company is being
bought out by a larger corporation at $25 a share. She
can buy common stock of the corporation now for $20

a share and in just six or eight weeks it will be worth $25 a share.

The first thing Monday morning, Shirley buys a hundred shares of that corporation's stock, but about a week later she notices the price of the stock has declined to $18. Although she is still confident of the $25 sell-out price, about a month later, when the price of the stock dropped to $15 a share, she becomes more concerned. She decides to discuss this confidential sell-out with her broker. He knows all about the possible sell-out and informs her the deal has fallen through. Shirley can't believe it.

She now has the choice of selling her stock for $15 a share and taking a loss or keeping the stock as a speculation, hoping its price will increase. After finding out the stock is rated B (below average) by Standard & Poor and it pays no dividends, she decides to sell and take a loss. Instead of getting information about a stock before she buys, she buys a stock on a rumor and then finds out the pertinent facts afterward—*she is surely wrong.*

Shirley Wright buys Common Stocks
Shirley locates a reputable broker working for a financially sound brokerage firm (see page 71). Although she can make judgments on her own when it comes to loaning money (buying bonds), she does not have the business background to make future projections for corporate earnings and must therefore rely on the recommendations from the research department of a sound brokerage firm. She realizes buying stock is more speculative than buying bonds; however, at this time, when investors are pessimistic and stock prices are depressed, she would like to buy stock.

Shirley calls her broker and asks for stock recommendations of the highest-quality stocks trading on the New York Stock Exchange. After reading the material she receives from the brokerage firm, she decides to speculate $4,200 by purchasing a hundred shares of AT&T common stock. Why? Because AT&T is a A+ stock, has a record of stable earnings, is a leader in its industry, has little competition and is selling well below ten times earnings. (Annual earnings for a share of AT&T stock at that time are $5.27 a share, so if she pays $42 a share this is about eight times its $5.27 annual earnings.) In addition, AT&T stock is currently yielding 8.19%.

Shirley calls her broker and places an order to buy a hundred shares of AT&T stock at a price of $42 a share or better (which means she will pay $42 a share or less). Her broker calls her back within the half hour to inform her that her order has been filled and that she has bought a hundred shares at $42 a share plus a commission charge of $72.

She is happy with her yield of over 8% and she hopes the price of AT&T stock will increase in the future. She realizes there is risk in buying any stock; however, she feels financially and emotionally prepared to assume this risk—*she is surely right.*

The following charts give you detailed information on common stock and preferred stock which may be helpful when you buy them or useful to compare them with other investments.

COMMON STOCKS

Type of Security

Shares of ownership in a corporation—registered certificates.

Denominations

Price of a share of stock.

Where to Buy and Sell

At a brokerage firm—no commission on stock offerings by underwriters and a negotiated commission at all other times.

Maturity Date

None.

Yield

Dividends are usually paid every 3 months if the directors of the corporation vote to pay them. This generally depends on the financial condition and earning power of the corporation. The first $100 received in dividends each year (per person) can be excluded from federal income tax.

Call Provision

Not callable.

Anticipated Profit or Loss (other than dividend income)	Profit can usually be anticipated if stock is sold after the corporation's earnings increase because other buyers are then willing to pay a higher price and a loss can generally be anticipated if earnings decrease because then buyers will usually pay a lower price.
Safety	Only as safe as the financial condition and earning ability of the issuing corporation.
How Much Liquidity?	Can be sold for cash every trading day for the price another buyer is willing to pay. Large stock issues of well-established companies that trade in large volume on the New York Stock Exchange normally bring relatively higher market resale prices.

PREFERRED STOCKS

Type of Security — Shares of ownership in a corporation usually limited to receiving a fixed dividend—registered certificates. However, convertible preferred stock can be exchanged for the common stock of the same company and cumulative preferred stock whose omitted dividends accumulate from one year to another must be paid before common stock dividends can be paid.

Denominations — Price of a share of stock.

Where to Buy and Sell — At a brokerage firm—no commission on stock offerings by underwriters and a negotiated commission at all other times.

Maturity Date — None.

Yield — A fixed dividend is usually paid every 3 months if the directors of the corporation vote to pay them. This usually depends on the financial condition and earning power of the corporation. The first $100 received in dividends each year (per person) can be excluded from federal income tax.

*C*all Provision	Usually callable.
*A*nticipated Profit or Loss (other than dividend income)	Anticipated profit if sold when interest rates decline in the future, and anticipated loss if sold when interest rates rise in the future.
*S*afety	Only as safe as the financial condition and earning ability of the issuing corporation; however, safer than common stock of the same corporation.
*H*ow Much Liquidity?	Can be sold for cash every trading day for the price another buyer is willing to pay. Large stock issues of well-established companies that trade in large volume on the New York Stock Exchange normally bring relatively higher market resale prices.

7

Should You Be
a Part Owner
of a Diversified Portfolio of Stocks and Bonds by Purchasing Shares of Mutual Funds? Investment Companies?

We have discussed how to buy stock and bonds on your own, but if you have a small amount of cash or you do not have the time or the know-how to buy securities on your own—that's when investment funds come into the picture. When you buy shares of investment funds (mutual funds and investment companies), you become a part owner of a large diversified portfolio of securities under professional management.

Both mutual funds and investment companies combine your money ($50, $100, $500 or more) with the money of thousands of other investors and use the total, say $1 million, to buy the securities of other corporations. For a limited amount of cash, you own part of a

209

large million-dollar portfolio consisting of fifty to a hundred different securities. This tends to reduce your risk of loss because the price decline of any one security has only a slight effect on the total value of this large diversified portfolio. This also tends, however, to reduce your chance of making large profits, which would be possible if you put all your money into one stock that subsequently doubled or tripled in price.

Investment funds hire professionals who do the research, select the securities and do all the paper work. For these services, funds charge an annual fee ranging from ½% to 1½% of your total investment (on a $500 investment you would be charged $2.50 to $7.50 a year). This fee is deducted quarterly before dividend income (produced by the securities in the fund's portfolio) and capital gains (produced if securities owned by the fund are sold for more than their original cost) are distributed to you. In case dividend income and capital gains are not adequate to pay these fees, funds sell securities held in their portfolio to pay them.

Funds offer you the choice of receiving your dividend income and capital gains in cash or in additional shares of the fund. Then, at the end of the year, funds mail you a statement listing whatever dividend income and capital gains were distributed that year. This amount must be declared on your tax return even if you have chosen to reinvest your money in additional shares of the fund.

Funds vary in the type of securities they buy. Most funds buy stocks (stock funds), some buy bonds (bond funds) and still others buy a combination of stocks and bonds (balanced funds). Furthermore, stock funds may specialize in certain types of stocks such as blue-chip stocks, growth stocks, energy stocks or even gold stocks, and bond funds may specialize in certain types of bonds such as government bonds, municipal bonds or even short-term money market securities, which include T-bills, commercial paper, bankers' acceptances and certificates of deposit (securities that come due in one year or less).

When you buy shares of a stock fund, you make or lose money according to how well the stocks in a fund's portfolio perform in the stock market. So, there is risk in buying shares of a stock fund. If you have a limited amount of cash, however, buying shares of a stock fund can be safer and sometimes more profitable than trying to buy stock on your own. A stock fund has a large diversified portfolio, which tends to reduce your risk of loss. If you have a relatively small amount of money to speculate, say $1,000, the brokerage fees you would pay to buy and sell several different stocks would reduce your profit by a large percentage. In addition, a stock fund provides professional expertise in selecting stocks. Past experience indicates that average investors do not have access to the same high-quality research that professionals do. Therefore, it can be well worth paying a ½% to 1½% annual fee to a stock fund for its professional management and diversification.

When you buy shares of a bond fund, you receive your share of the income produced by the bonds in the fund's portfolio. If you have less than $1,000 to invest, you may want to buy shares of a bond fund because buying bonds on your own usually requires a minimum of $1,000. In addition, if you have less than $10,000 when short-term interest rates are very high (as in 1974), you may want to buy shares of a money market fund. Otherwise, buying shares of a bond fund is usually not as profitable as buying bonds on your own. Why? Because you do not need professional expertise for a bond portfolio. Bonds with "like" ratings and "like" maturity dates generally pay the same amount of income, so it would be foolish for you to pay ½% to 1½% in an annual fee to a bond fund since this reduces your income.

Since all funds are not equally successful, how do you select the fund more likely to do a good job for you? Funds that have performed well in the past are more likely to do well in the future. *Forbes* magazine's annual mutual fund issue and Weisenberger's annual book, *Investment Companies,* list the last ten-year performance records of investment funds. These publications can be found in most public libraries.

Both types of investment funds, mutual funds and investment companies, operate the same way in that they both raise the money they need to go into business by selling a large issue of shares to the investing public, and they both hire professional management to reinvest this money in the securities of other corporations. But mutual funds and investment companies also differ. Even after the original offering, on any trading day, mutual funds sell new shares to investors and also repurchase previously issued shares from investors. So, the number of shares issued by mutual funds is unlimited or "open," which is why the trade refers to mutual funds as open-end funds.

By contrast, after the original offering, investment companies neither sell new shares to investors nor repurchase their previously issued shares from investors. Instead, investors buy and sell shares of investment companies in the stock market just as they buy and sell all other corporate stock. So, the number of shares issued by investment companies is fixed, or "closed," after the original offering, which is why the trade refers to investment companies as closed-end funds.

MUTUAL FUNDS (OPEN-END FUNDS)

Mutual funds sell shares and also repurchase shares every business day. Funds figure the amount of net assets they own for each outstanding share at least once a day. The net asset value of one share of a mutual fund is determined by adding together the value of the fund's assets (the securities the fund owns and its cash), subtracting any expenses and dividing this total by the number of shares outstanding. Funds usually repurchase their shares whenever you want to sell them at their net asset value; however, not all funds sell you shares when you want to buy them at their net asset value.

Mutual funds that are load funds sell shares through stockbrokers and sales organizations. Load funds charge more than net asset value for their shares because you must assume the "load" of paying a sales commission of about 8% to 9%. The commission is added to the net asset value of each share you buy. In other words, if the net asset value of a share is $10, and there is an 8% load charge (80¢), you pay $10.80 for that share. So, if you invest $1,000, $80 goes to the salesperson immediately and the remaining $920 buys ninety-two shares in the fund.

Mutual funds that are no-load funds sell shares directly to you. No-load funds charge you only the net asset value to buy shares because there is "no-load" for you to assume, that is, there is no broker or salesperson involved and so there is no sales charge. Naturally, brokers and fund salespeople don't talk about no-load funds, and probably the only way you would hear about them is through other investors. All the money you invest in no-load mutual fund shares goes directly for shares of the fund. In other words, if the net asset value of a share in a no-load fund is $10, you pay $10 for that share. So, if you invest $1,000, you buy 100 shares.

Obviously, you get more value when you buy no-load mutual funds and pay no sales charge. But since no salespeople will come looking for you, you must take the initiative yourself. You can write to the No-Load

Mutual Fund Association (a nonprofit association), Valley Forge, Pennsylvania 19481, for a list of the names and addresses of no-load mutual funds. Then you can write directly to any no-load mutual fund for additional information or to buy shares in the fund.

The prices of shares of mutual funds are published daily in most city newspapers and in the *Wall Street Journal*. For example,

	NAV or Sell	Offer Price Buy
Aetna Fd	11.53	12.60
Afuture Fd	8.33	NL

Let's read this together. *NAV* stands for *N*et *A*sset *V*alue and the amount you receive for each share you *Sell* back to the fund. *Offer* is the price you pay for each share you *Buy* from a fund. *Aetna Fund* is a load fund because the price to buy a share is $12.60, which is $1.07 more than the price you receive when you sell a share back to the fund—$11.53. The $1.07 is the sales charge that goes to the broker or fund salesperson. *Afuture Fund* is a no-load fund, and under *Buy* you see the initials *NL,* which stand for no-load and mean there is no sales charge. So, the price you pay to buy a share is $8.33, the same price you receive when you sell a share to a no-load fund.

INVESTMENT COMPANIES (CLOSED-END FUNDS)

Investment companies originally sell a specific number of shares of stock to raise the money they need to go into business. They then reinvest the money they raise in the securities of other corporations. Subsequent to this, investment companies neither sell new shares nor repurchase outstanding shares. Therefore, if you want to buy or sell shares of investment companies after their original offering, you buy or sell them from other investors through your broker (in the stock market). The stocks of investment companies trade on major exchanges and in the over-the-counter market, and you pay the same brokerage fees as you do to buy other corporate stocks (about 2%).

Since investment company stocks trade in the stock market, their market price is determined by their supply in relation to their demand rather than by their net asset value like mutual fund shares. As a result, shares of investment company stocks may sell for more than net asset value (at a premium) or for less than net asset value (at a discount).

No one is sure why shares of investment company stocks so frequently sell for less than their net asset value. Some suspect there is less demand for these shares of stocks because most investors do not know about them, pointing out that brokers would rather promote shares of load mutual funds that pay them a sales commission of 8% or 9% than promote the stocks of investment companies that pay them only a regular brokerage fee of 2%. Whatever the reason, when the stocks of investment companies with good management sell at large discounts from their net asset value, they may be considered buying opportunities for anyone that wants to speculate in stocks.

Every Monday the *Wall Street Journal,* under the heading Closed-end Funds (the other name for investment companies), lists all the investment companies, their net asset value per share (N. A.), and the percentage a share sells above or below its net asset value. Included in this list are Tri-Continental Corporation and The Lehman Corporation, two of the largest investment companies.

You can write to the Closed-End Investment Com-

pany Association, 330 Madison Avenue, New York City,
New York, 10017, for additional information about investment companies, and you can ask your broker for
the individual Standard & Poor stock sheet for any investment company stock that interests you.

Since shares of investment company stocks trade just
like other corporate stocks, their prices are also listed
on major exchanges and in the over-the-counter market.

MY CASH Checklist for Mutual Funds and Investment Companies

You can buy stocks and bonds on your own or you can
buy shares of mutual funds and investment companies
and become a part owner of the stocks and bonds they
hold in their diversified portfolios. Let's briefly go over
the highlights of mutual funds and investment companies by using the MY CASH checklist.

Shares of mutual funds and investment companies
have no *M*aturity dates. Although mutual funds generally repay the net asset value of your shares whenever
you want to sell them, they do not promise to pay the
original cost of your shares on any date in the future.
The *Y*ields mutual fund and investment company
shares pay are unpredictable and vary from year to
year depending upon what the securities in their portfolios yield. These yields are reduced by management
fees and sometimes by a sales charge. Shares of mutual
funds and investment companies are not *C*allable. You
can usually *A*nticipate a profit if the securities owned
by the investment fund rise in price and you can generally anticipate a loss if their securities decline in price.
The *S*afety of investment funds depends upon the
financial condition of the corporations issuing the different securities they own. *H*ow much liquidity? Although you can normally receive cash at any time for
both mutual fund shares and investment company

stocks, mutual fund shares offer more liquidity because they are redeemable for their current net asset value, whereas the market price for shares of investment company stocks depends on their supply and demand in the stock market, which means they may be worth more or less than the current net asset value (usually less).

Shirley Wright Buys Shares of an Investment Fund

Shirley Wright owns a hundred shares of AT&T stock which she bought primarily for income. Now she wants to speculate in growth stocks, but she does not have the business background to judge the future growth potential of a corporation. She therefore decides that rather than buying the shares of a few different corporations on her own, she will buy shares of a growth stock fund to take advantage of its diversification and its professional management.

Shirley would like to buy the stock of an investment company selling for less than its net asset value (at a discount). So, she checks Monday's *Wall Street Journal* under the heading Closed-end Funds where she finds the stocks of six investment companies are currently selling for less than their net asset value. She then goes to the library to check the last ten-year performances of these six investment companies in *Forbes* magazine's annual mutual fund issue and finds that two of the six companies have excellent past records.

Now, Shirley calls her broker who suggests she buy shares in a load mutual fund which she can redeem every business day at net asset value rather than buy shares in an investment company. She knows that if she buys shares in a load mutual fund, she must pay her broker a sales commission of about 8% to 9%, which means the $5,000 she has to invest buys only $4,550 worth of assets because $450 goes to the broker. However, she also knows that if she buys the stocks of either of the investment companies selling for 18% less than their net asset value, she will receive about $5,800 worth of assets for her $5,000 (even after deducting the regular brokerage fee of 2%). She may not of course be able to sell these shares for $5,800, but she will receive the dividend income as well as capital gains produced by $5,800 worth of assets.

She asks her broker to mail the Standard & Poor stock sheets on the two investment companies that interest her. These write-ups help her narrow her choice to the one company whose portfolio of stocks is the type she prefers, well-established growth companies. She then calls her broker and places an order to buy 200 shares of stock in this investment company, which trades on the New York Stock Exchange. Her order was executed at $24 a share plus $93 in brokerage fees for a total cost of $4,893.

A year later, the price of this investment company stock had increased to $30 a share, very close to its current net asset value. Shirley bought shares of investment company stock to receive the dividend income and capital gains from $5,800 worth of assets for the discount price of $4,893. Now, she decides to sell these shares because they are no longer selling at a large discount from their net asset value.

Shirley sells her 200 shares at $30 a share and receives $5,885, after deducting $109 in commission charges and a $5 sales tax. She pays only the minimum sales tax of $5 because she has signed a New York State tax waiver which allows nonresidents of the state to pay a lower sales tax on the securities they sell. Her profit from this sale is $992 (her $5,885 sales price less her $4,893 purchase price). This profit is taxed at one-half the ordinary income tax rate (the capital gains rate). In addition, she has received $174 in dividend income and $58 in capital gains from the investment company during the year she owned the stock. This is the total return of $1,224 on her $4,893 speculation in investment company stock for an annual yield of 24%.

Shirley realizes there is risk in stock investments (even in buying shares of a stock fund); however, she can well afford this risk. She also realizes the additional risk can be rewarded by substantial gain—*she is surely right.*

8

Can You Emotionally and
Financially Afford to
Risk Money to Buy
Warrants?
Options?
Commodity Futures?

We have already discussed buying and selling stocks
and bonds. However, there are other ways to make
money in the securities market. You can also buy and
sell warrants, options and commodity futures, which
were popular speculations in the 1970s.

Warrants and options allow you to profit from stock
price fluctuations at just a fraction of the cost of buying
stocks, and commodity futures allow you to profit from
price fluctuations of large quantities of commodities
(such as wheat, sugar or even foreign currencies) with
only a small down payment. Although warrants, options
and commodity futures are usually not recommended
for the average investor, if you have savings to risk

(money you can afford to lose that will not jeopardize the financial well-being of yourself or your family), and if risking money does not cause you great anxiety or lure you on to excessive gambling, then you may be interested in trying these speculations.

Speculators risk savings to buy warrants, options and commodity futures because they offer leverage; that is, a relatively small amount of money can produce a large percentage of profit. The more leverage speculators want, the more risk they must be willing to assume.

These speculations are talked about so often that even though you may not be interested in trying them, you may want to know what they offer and how they trade. Should you decide to buy warrants, options or commodity futures, be sure to consult an expert in each of these fields. Furthermore, it is of utmost importance that you too become knowledgeable in that field. Although a broker can advise you, the final decision is yours to make because it is your judgment that will determine if you make or lose money.

WARRANTS

What are warrants? Warrants are similar to stockholders' rights (see page 195) in that they give you the right to buy shares of stock directly from a corporation at a fixed price for a long period of time (usually up to twenty years). Warrants have been issued by only a few dozen corporations and are originally included as a free bonus with new issues of stocks or bonds.

Corporations like to issue warrants because they attract more buyers for their new issues of stocks and bonds. In addition, warrants allow corporations to raise more money in the future because if investors exercise their warrants (use them to buy shares of stock), corporations sell additional shares of stock.

Investors like warrants because if the price of the underlying stock (the stock the warrant permits you to buy) rises, they can use their warrants to buy shares of that stock below their market price. Furthermore, they can sell warrants to other speculators in the stock market just as they would sell shares of stock. In other words, during their lifetime, warrants become securities themselves and trade actively on major exchanges and in the over-the-counter market.

The market price for warrants is only a fraction of the cost of the underlying stock. After all, a warrant is only permission to buy that stock at a fixed price. But if the market price of the underlying stock rises, warrants that allow you to buy that stock for less than the market price become more valuable and, therefore, they too rise in price. On the other hand, if the market price of the underlying stock declines, warrants that allow you to buy that stock for more than the market price become less valuable and, therefore, they too decline in price. In addition, the longer the time to the warrants' expiration date, the longer the time warrants allow you to profit from a price rise of the underlying stock— which makes them more valuable; whereas, the shorter the time to their expiration date, the shorter the time warrants allow you to profit from a price rise—which makes them less valuable. And, of course, when warrants expire they become worthless.

To get an idea of how warrants work, let's use AT&T warrants issued as a bonus with an AT&T bond issue in 1970 as an example. Each warrant gave the owner the right to buy one share of AT&T stock at $52 a share for five years (1970 to 1975). In other words, one warrant plus $52 in cash would buy one share of AT&T stock directly from AT&T without paying a brokerage fee. If all the 31.3 million warrants issued were exercised (that is, used to buy shares of stock), AT&T would raise $1.57 billion (after deducting the fees they paid) from the sale of additional shares of stock.

AT&T warrants traded actively on the New York Stock Exchange and their market prices fluctuated primarily with the price of AT&T stock. When the stock was selling for about $39 a share, the warrants sold for 37½¢ each; and when the stock sold for $75 a share, then the warrants were more valuable and sold for $13 each.

Sometimes speculators bought AT&T warrants in anticipation of actually buying AT&T stock in the future. That way, they were able to buy AT&T stock at $52 a share any time before the warrants expired in 1975. Most times, however, speculators bought AT&T warrants in anticipation of making a profit from a price rise of the warrants themselves. Furthermore, when the price of AT&T stock rose, they could make a larger percentage of profit buying warrants than they could by using the same amount of money to buy shares of AT&T stock. For example, when AT&T warrants were selling for 37½¢ each, you could buy 1,000 warrants for $375. At the same time AT&T stock was selling for $39 a share, so you could buy ten shares for about $390. Subsequently, when the price of AT&T stock rose to $75 a share, the price of the warrants rose to $13 each. Then, 1,000 warrants could be sold for $13,000 for a profit of $12,627 (less commission), whereas ten shares of AT&T stock could be sold for only $750 for a profit of $360 (less commission)—quite a difference!

Although this sounds tempting, remember that warrants pay no dividends, and that if the price of AT&T stock had not risen before the warrants expired in 1975, you would probably have lost some or all of the $375 you paid for the warrants (depending upon what other investors would pay for them in the stock market). On the other hand, the ten shares of AT&T stock would have paid you dividends, and even if the price of AT&T stock had not risen, your shares would still be worth the

$390 you paid for them. What makes warrants an attractive speculation is they limit your risk to the small amount you pay to buy them (if the price of a stock does not rise), and yet there is no limit to the amount of profit you can make (if the price of the stock does rise).

By coincidence, in 1975, just one day before AT&T warrants expired, the price of AT&T stock was the warrant exercise price of $52 a share. On that day, thousands of AT&T warrants traded for 8¢ each, even though they would expire and become worthless the next day. Why? Because investors found paying a relatively small brokerage fee plus 8¢ for the warrants (which they could use to buy shares of AT&T stock at $52 a share directly from AT&T) was cheaper than paying the larger brokerage fee required to buy AT&T stock at $52 a share on the New York Stock Exchange.

There are other aspects of dealing with warrants too complicated to include in this brief discussion, for example, buying warrants and at the same time short selling the same stock. Furthermore, the value of warrants can be adversely affected by stock splits, stock dividends and call provisions. Therefore, be advised again: Before you buy warrants, consult a broker that specializes in the sale of warrants who will give you more detailed information.

MY CASH Checklist for Warrants
Let's go over the highlights of warrants by using the MY CASH checklist. Warrants usually have original *M*aturity dates of up to twenty years. They pay no dividends, so offer no annual *Y*ield. Some warrants are *C*allable and call provisions should be checked before they are purchased. You can usually *A*nticipate a profit if the price of the underlying stock rises and you can anticipate a loss if the price of the underlying stock declines; however, you can never lose more than the original cost of the warrants. There is no *S*afety factor

because you are risking your money to profit from price increases of the underlying stock. *H*ow much liquidity for warrants? You can normally call your broker and sell warrants for cash if they have value, but warrants sold on major exchanges and in large volume usually bring relatively better market resale prices.

Shirley Wright Buys Warrants

Shirley Wright owns a hundred shares of AT&T stock and feels that at this time AT&T stock offers exceptional value. As a result, she becomes interested in speculating a few hundred dollars in AT&T warrants because they offer her an inexpensive way to profit from the price rise of AT&T stock. She also understands the risk she is taking: If AT&T stock does not rise in price before the warrants expire, she may lose the money she pays for them. However, since this loss will not affect her financial well-being, she thinks she would like to buy AT&T warrants.

She calls the brokerage firm and speaks to the broker that specializes in trading warrants. She finds out AT&T warrants are selling for 40¢ each, they expire in one year and they give her the right to buy one share of AT&T stock at $52 a share (AT&T stock is currently selling at $40 a share). Shirley decides to buy 1,000 AT&T warrants and pays $400 plus commission.

Nine months later, when AT&T stock is selling for $53 a share, the warrants are selling for $3 each. Shirley decides to take her profit because she thinks the price of AT&T shares will probably not rise much more (if any) before the warrants expire. She sells her warrants and receives $3,000 (less commission).

Shirley appreciates the leverage these warrants offered her. By risking $400, she is able to make a $2,600 profit, or a gain of over 600%—*she is surely right.*

OPTIONS

Options, like warrants, give you permission to buy
shares of stock at a fixed price for a definite period of
time, and they too cost only a fraction of the price of the
underlying stock (about 5% to 15% of the market value
of that stock). However, options differ from warrants in
that they are issued by private individuals rather than
by corporations. Thousands of individuals issue options
for hundreds of different stocks, whereas only a few
dozen corporations issue warrants for a few dozen
stocks. Individuals are only willing to issue options that
give you permission to buy stock at a fixed price generally for the short period of time of one year or less,
whereas corporations are willing to issue warrants that
give you permission to buy stock at a fixed price for the
long period of time of up to twenty years. Although
options expire in the short time of one year or less, they
still allow you to do more things than warrants. Why?
Because individuals are willing to issue two types of
options. You can buy options, like warrants, that allow
you to make a profit if the price of a stock rises (call
options), but you can also buy options that allow you to
make a profit if the price of the stock declines (put
options). Let's see how the two types of options work.

When you buy a call option, you pay another individual a fee (a premium), and in return this individual
agrees to sell you a hundred shares of a particular stock
at a fixed price (usually the current market price) usually for up to one year. If the price of the stock rises, you
make a profit because you can buy the stock from the
individual who issued your option for a price less than
the current market price, and then you can sell the
same stock in the stock market at the current higher
market price.

When you buy a put option, you pay another individual a fee, and in return this individual agrees to buy a hundred shares of a particular stock from you at a fixed price (usually the current market price) generally for up to one year. If the price of that stock declines, you make a profit because you can sell the stock to the individual who issued your option for a price higher than the current market price, and then you can buy the same stock in the stock market at the lower current market price.

Exchange-Traded Options

For over fifty years, put and call options have been trading in the over-the-counter market. Brokers find private individuals who, for a fee (a premium), are willing to issue (write) options. In addition, the brokerage firm guarantees every option transaction. In case the writers of the options do not keep their word, the brokerage firm itself will honor the option.

Over-the-counter options do not trade actively. Why? Because the only way you can make a profit or limit a loss on an over-the-counter option is to actually buy and sell (or sell and buy) the underlying hundred shares of stock. Then, of course, your profit is reduced greatly by the two large brokerage fees you must pay.

In the mid-1970s, for the first time, the Chicago Board Option Exchange (CBOE), the American Stock Exchange (AMEX) and the Pacific Stock Exchange (PSE) provided markets where call options themselves could be bought and sold. In other words, you no longer have to buy and sell the hundred shares of the underlying stock in the stock market in order to make a profit or to limit your loss on an option. Instead, exchange-traded options trade as securities themselves. Now you can buy and sell options on the option exchanges for relatively small brokerage fees because options themselves cost only a fraction of the cost of the hundred underlying shares of stock (5% to 15%).

In the mid-1970s, option exchanges offered call options for most of the actively traded stocks listed on the New York Stock Exchange, but they did not trade put options. In the future, however, option exchanges will probably trade put options as well.

The market price you pay for an option is the premium (the fee that goes to the individual that writes the option). This premium fluctuates with the price of the underlying stock and with the length of time to the option's expiration date (like the market price for warrants, see page 222).

Like warrants, call options are sometimes bought to fix the price of the underlying stock in anticipation of buying that stock in the future, but most times call options are bought in anticipation of making a profit from the price rise of the option itself. If the price of a stock rises, you can make a larger percentage of profit by purchasing an option than you can by using an equal amount of money to buy shares of the underlying stock (like warrants, see the AT&T example on page 223).

The exchanges have standardized the expiration dates for options to make it easier for them to match the buy and sell orders for the hundreds of different options. If you buy an exchange-traded option, you always have the choice of three specific expiration dates. For example, if in December you decide to buy an AT&T option, you would have the choice of buying an option expiring the end of January, the end of April or the end of July (these dates are preset by the option exchange).

Furthermore, option exchanges have their own jargon, which you should be familiar with. Let's assume, in December, AT&T stock was selling for $45 a share and you called your broker to buy an AT&T call option. You would probably hear the following reply, "I can offer you an AT&T January 45 call for 1, an April 45 call for 1½ and a July 45 call for 2½". This means you have the choice of three call options to buy AT&T stock at $45 a share—the first call option expires at the end of January and you pay a premium of $1 a share; the second call option expires at the end of April and you pay a premium of $1.50 a share; and the third call option expires the end of July and you pay a premium of $2.50 a share. Since each option is for a hundred shares, your total premium would be $100, $150 or $250 (plus commission).

To repeat, exchange-traded options trade just like shares of stock, and you do not have to exercise them to make a profit or to limit a loss. Furthermore, option traders generally take their profits (or limit their losses) by buying and selling options on exchanges rather than by exercising options to actually buy the stock. Indeed, since most options are not exercised, more and more brokerage firms are encouraging customers (private individuals) to consider the other side of the option market—issuing options (writing them).

Writing Exchange-Traded Call Options
When call options are not exercised, the option writers make the money because they are paid a premium (which they keep) and they also keep their stock, which they had agreed to sell for a fixed price. Thus, if you own stock and want to make additional income, you may want to consider writing options.

It is also possible to write call options without owning the stock. These are called uncovered ("naked") options because you do not own the stock to cover them. This is riskier than buying options or selling covered options.

When you buy an option, all you can lose is the price of the option, the so-called premium. When you sell a covered option, all you can lose is the paper gain the stock has made above your agreed selling price; however, when you sell an uncovered option without owning the stock and the price of the stock rises rapidly, your possible loss can be considerable. As the seller of the option, you can be called upon to deliver stock and you will be forced to buy that stock in the open market at whatever its market price is at that time.

The Spread

You buy options when you think the price of stock will rise sharply in the near future and you write options when you think the price of stock will stay the same or decline a little in the near future, but what do you do if you are uncertain or if you want to limit losses on options? That's when you look for what is called the spread.

The spread is a complicated transaction that involves buying and selling options of the same stock, stock that you do not own. The idea is that the money lost on one side will be made up with a possible profit on the other side, but spreads do not always work that way. By using the spread, you are likely to make money if the stock stays the same, goes up or goes down a little, and supposedly the only time you can lose is if the stock goes up or down too much.

There are bull spreads, bear spreads, time spreads, vertical spreads and even money spreads. These are complex techniques that require professional expertise.

Many other considerations, such as commission rates and tax ramifications, have not been discussed. Options are a complicated investment strategy that require the know-how of experts. If they interest you, consult the option expert in your brokerage firm. Skeptics think options are a passing fad, but experts—those who are educating themselves in every aspect of option trading—feel the option market will continue to grow.

MY CASH Checklist for Exchange-traded Call Options

Let's review call options traded on the exchanges by using the MY CASH checklist. Since you can be the buyer of a call option or the seller (writer) of a call option, this checklist will be two-sided. Call options usually have original *M*aturities of less than one year. Buyers of options receive no *Y*ield, whereas sellers receive yield from the premium income. Call options are not *C*allable. Buyers of options *A*nticipate making a profit from the price rise of the underlying stock, but should the price of the stock decline, they can never lose more than the premiums they paid for the options. Sellers of options ordinarily own the stock, so their anticipated profit or loss is made from owning the stock and not from writing the options. There is no *S*afety factor in buying or selling options. Buyers of options risk their money solely to profit from the price increases in the underlying stock, and sellers generally own the stock so their safety factor is determined by the safety of the stock itself. *H*ow much liquidity for call options? Buyers of call options can normally sell their options for cash whenever an option has value. Sellers have already sold their options when they write the contracts, but they can neutralize their position by buying a like call option on the exchange whenever they choose to.

Shirley Wright Writes an Option

Shirley owns a hundred shares of AT&T stock. She believes the price of AT&T stock will not rise or decline very much for the next several months, so she decides to write an option. That way, she receives premium income, and if her judgment proves right, she will also be able to keep her AT&T stock.

After she consults with the option expert in her brokerage firm, she writes a six-month call option on her hundred shares of AT&T stock at the current market price of $50 a share and receives a $200 premium. Now if the buyer exercises this option before the six-month period, Shirley must sell her hundred shares of AT&T stock at $50 a share, and she also keeps the $2 a share premium she receives. So, she actually receives $52 a share for her stock, or $2 more than its current market price. On the other hand, if the buyer of the option does not exercise the option, which is more likely, she pockets the $200 premium and also keeps her hundred shares of AT&T stock.

AT&T stock did not rise in price in the next six months; in fact, it declined to $48 a share. Naturally, the buyer did not exercise the option to buy AT&T stock at $50 a share when AT&T stock sold for only $48 a share on the New York Stock Exchange. As a result, Shirley keeps the $200 premium, which has been earning interest in her savings account since she originally sold the option six months ago. Thus, in six months she has received an income of $345 from her hundred shares of AT&T stock—$170 from two quarterly dividends and $175 ($200 premium minus $25 commission) for writing the option—*she is surely right.*

COMMODITY FUTURES

"SUGAR PRICES DROP THE LIMIT!" "GOLD PRICES SOAR!" "TRADING IN COCOA FUTURES TEMPORARILY HALTED!"

These are the daily happenings in the commodity futures market. If you are looking for action and can afford to risk several thousand dollars in anticipation of making enormous profits, the commodity futures market may interest you.

Commodity futures are an entirely different type of speculation. You actually buy and sell large quantities of commodities for delivery to you on a date in the future (delivery date) by making a small down payment (5% to 20% of the total cost). This small down payment allows you to profit from the price fluctuation of large quantities of commodities (carload lots), which in turn magnifies both your profits and your losses.

You buy and sell commodity futures solely in anticipation of making profits from their volatile price fluctuations. Since commodity futures pay no dividends, and since you have no use for carloads of commodities such as sugar, wheat or even pork bellies, you take your profit (or loss) from commodity futures before their delivery date.

Although the commodity exchanges limit how much the price of each commodity can fluctuate in one trading day, there are times when commodities temporarily do not trade. As a result, you can be locked into a commodity future for many days. By the time the commodity trades again, the daily price fluctuations for that period of time can work to your advantage and increase your profit sharply or can work to your disadvantage and increase your loss sharply. However, you can always liquidate commodity futures at some price before their delivery date.

But we are getting a little ahead of the commodity futures story, so let's go back and start at the beginning: Commodities are basic products essential for all aspects of American commerce (industrial staples) and include foods (such as sugar and pork bellies), grains (such as wheat, corn, rye), fats and oils (such as peanut oil, lard, soybean oil), metals (such as silver, gold, copper) and even foreign currencies (such as Swiss francs, German marks, British pounds).

Commodities are bought and sold in two different markets: the commodity cash market and the commodity futures market. The cash market (referred to as the "actual" or "spot" market) is where anyone can buy a small amount of corn for chicken feed or where grain elevator operators buy five carloads of wheat directly from farmers. The buyers and sellers usually meet face to face and agree upon the grade, the price and the delivery date of the commodity. The commodities are generally delivered immediately, although they also can be for future delivery. You only buy commodities in the cash market that you plan to use. In other words, buying commodities in the cash market is much like buying farm products at a farmer's market.

The futures market is a commodity exchange where you trade commodities in anticipation of making money from commodities you do not plan to use. You buy and sell large fixed quantities of commodities at stated prices for future delivery (up to eighteen months). The minimum amount of a commodity you can buy on a commodity exchange is one contract. Since early contracts were for agricultural products, the minimum commodity contract was standardized to be the amount needed to fill a railroad car. Subsequently, when other commodities were listed for trading, the exchanges set their contracts for equally large quantities, although not necessarily railroad carloads. For example, one wheat futures contract is for 5,000 bushels of wheat, one sugar futures contract is for 112,000 pounds of sugar and one Swiss franc futures contract is for 250,000 Swiss francs. By 1975, there were over forty commodities trading on more than a dozen different commodity exchanges.

You never see the party on the other side of a futures contract. Instead, the clearing house of the commodity exchange matches all the buy and sell orders and guarantees both the integrity and the delivery of every contract.

Most of the time future prices for commodities are slightly higher than cash prices because of the carrying costs to a future month, such as insurance, storage and interest charges. For example, in December, if the cash price for sugar is 13¢ a pound, the future price for sugar, say, for July delivery, might be ¼¢ more, or 13¼¢ a pound. Occasionally, when enough buyers and sellers believe the price of a particular commodity will decline in the future, even when its carrying costs are added on, the future price may be lower than the cash price.

A brief look into the history of commodity futures will give you a better understanding of how they work and what they offer.

Early American businesspeople developed what was known as a "to-arrive" contract. The seller would assure delivery of his goods at a fixed price at a future date. For example, a miller would assure the delivery of flour to a baker at a fixed price for delivery in three months. In turn, the baker could then fix the price of bread for three months in the future.

The miller, however, could not afford to tie up his cash for three months to buy the wheat to process this order (say, 20,000 bushels of wheat) nor did he have adequate storage for this wheat. Thus, the miller had no price protection.

At first, this price risk was minimal, but as American business expanded, the demand for wheat (as well as for other commodities) increased. Since the supply of wheat was uncertain, affected as it is by many uncontrollable factors such as adverse weather conditions, strikes, wars and even political situations, and the demand was great, this caused the price of wheat to fluctuate so violently that the miller could no longer afford to give the "to-arrive" protection to the baker.

The volatility of commodity prices created the need for commodity futures markets (commodity exchanges), which came into the picture at this point. The exchanges organized the trading of commodity futures to entice speculators (the general public, who had no use for large quantities of these commodities) into the commodity market to make commodity trading more active, which, in turn, would make commodity futures more liquid. In addition, speculators motivated by making large profits from the wide price fluctuations of commodities would assume the price risks businesspeople sought to avoid.

The exchanges make commodity futures attractive speculations by charging low commissions ($30 to $70, which includes the charges for both buying and selling a commodity future) and by requiring the small down payment of 5% to 20% with no interest payable on the balance of the money for the total contract. Furthermore, even before you liquidate commodity futures, the clearing house of the exchange allows you to withdraw profits above the required small down payment because the down payment is only a security deposit to protect the broker from incurring any losses on your commodity contract. In other words, whenever commodity future contracts increase in value, you are allowed to withdraw cash. Whenever commodity future contracts decrease in value, however, you have to come up with additional cash. If you do not come up with additional cash (or collateral) immediately, the broker can liquidate your contract, and you are legally responsible for losses which may be more or less than your small down payment.

Commodity exchanges offer businesspeople a way to protect themselves against loss from the price fluctuations of the commodities they use in their business. This is called "hedging" and these businesspeople are referred to by the trade as "hedgers." Hedgers buy commodity futures to fix the price of commodities they will need to fill orders sold for future delivery, and they sell commodity futures to fix the price of inventory they own for which they have no future orders.

Hedgers are satisfied with the normal profits from

processing, manufacturing or marketing the various commodities. So, they buy and sell commodity futures to fix the price of commodities they use rather than to make a profit or take a loss. For example, the miller can fix the price of flour he sells to the baker for delivery in three months by purchasing four wheat future contracts (5,000 bushels each) at a fixed price with a small down payment and no storage problems.

Commodity exchanges offer speculators, who have no use for large quantities of commodities, the chance of making profits from their price changes. They buy commodity futures when they believe the price of a commodity will rise in the future, and they sell commodity futures when they believe the price of a commodity will decline in the future. Suppose, for example, in July, you believed the price of sugar would rise in the next nine months. You could call your broker and buy one sugar futures contract (112,000 pounds of sugar) at 23¢ a pound ($25,760 total) for March delivery (called March sugar). You would be required to give your broker a security deposit of about 10% of the total value of the March sugar contract you bought, or $2,576. When the price of a sugar contract (or any other commodity contract) moves in your favor, you are allowed to withdraw the profit from your contract without selling it. You can either keep the cash or use it to buy additional sugar contracts.

Suppose that six months after you bought the sugar contract (in January) you sold your one original March contract when the price of sugar was 44¢ a pound. Then, in just six months, on a down payment of $2,576, you would have made a profit of $23,458 (buying the contract for $25,760 and subsequently selling it for $49,820 less $62 commission). Furthermore, had you used the cash you were allowed to withdraw to buy additional sugar futures and also sold them at this time, you would have pyramided your original $2,576 down payment to several hundred thousand dollars. Of course, had the reverse happened and the price of sugar declined, you would have lost money, perhaps even more than your small security deposit. This would have occurred because sometimes commodities do not trade, which may force you to take large losses before you can liquidate your commodity future.

You can also sell commodity futures without owning the commodity when you believe the price of a commodity will decline in the future. Should the price of that commodity then decline (as you predicted), you make a profit by subsequently buying a commodity contract back at a lower price. But should the price of that commodity then rise, you take a loss because you must subsequently buy a commodity contract back at a higher price by delivery date.

Before you buy or sell commodity futures and assume the price risks businesspeople seek to avoid, you should understand the workings of commodity markets, make an in-depth study of the commodity you want to trade and have enough money to risk ($7,500 to $10,000 is usually the recommended minimum because of the volatile price fluctuations of commodities). If you are interested in trading commodities, locate an experienced and reputable commodity broker, one who has made a lifetime study of commodity trading. Your broker can explain commodity futures transactions in more detail and can also give you publications with current information about the commodity markets as well as about the commodities themselves.

We have discussed the basic commodity futures transactions but we have not taken into consideration tax ramifications or the more complicated techniques of spreads and straddles used to limit your risk.

MY CASH Checklist for Commodity Futures

Let's review the highlights of commodity futures trading for both speculators and hedgers by using the MY CASH checklist. The *M*aturity date for commodity futures is their delivery date. Commodity futures pay no annual *Y*ield and are not *C*allable. When speculators trade commodity futures, they *A*nticipate a profit if the price for that commodity moves the way they predicted, and they anticipate a loss if the price of that commodity does not move the way they predicted. Hedgers anticipate no profit and no loss because they are only fixing the price of specific commodities they use. There is no *S*afety factor for speculators when trading commodity futures because they are risking their money solely to profit from the volatile price fluctuations in the commodity, whereas the hedgers have the safety of price insurance for that commodity. *H*ow much liquidity for commodity futures? This varies; sometimes commodity futures trade actively and can be sold or bought back for cash immediately, whereas at other times trading is limited, making it impossible to trade at reasonable prices. You should consult an expert on this.

Shirley Wright Considers Commodity Futures Trading

Shirley Wright decides to find out more about commodity futures trading by locating an experienced commodity broker. She calls her brokerage firm and finds out there is a broker in the firm who is a commodity expert and has been schooled in every aspect of commodity futures trading.

She makes an appointment to discuss commodity futures. The broker explains the workings of the commodity market and the various ways to limit the risk of commodity futures trading and tells her about many of the actively traded commodities.

Shirley decides she is most interested in trading future contracts of wheat because the contract is relatively small in total cost and trades actively. The broker gives her U.S. government reports, brokerage firm pamphlets and commodity exchange pamphlets which provide information about the various factors that affect the price of wheat.

After she carefully studies all this information, she decides to test her ability to predict the future price of wheat by hypothetically trading wheat futures for several months. At the end of that time, she will decide if she is willing to risk money in trading commodity futures of wheat—*she is surely right.*

9

Do Your Dollars Need the Inflation Protection of Silver and/or Gold Coins? Real Estate?

Inflation is a disease that eats away at the value of paper dollars. In the mid-1970s, everyone was aware of the fact that dollars were buying less and less groceries, but not everyone was aware that inflation was also eating away at the buying power of savings invested in paper assets (bank accounts, bond and stocks). In other words, the money you deposited in banks or in bonds would buy less in the future when you withdrew that money to spend. If inflation is moderate, the money invested in common stocks usually increases in value faster than the rate of inflation; however, this is not true with severe inflation, which restricts corporate profits (lowers earnings) and, in turn, causes stock prices to decline. Therefore, whenever the annual rate of inflation is greater than the rate of return produced by paper assets, you need other ways to protect the buying power of your savings.

Historically, silver coins, gold coins and real estate have offered a way to protect the buying power of savings during periods of severe inflation because they

have appreciated in value faster than the rate of inflation. For example, from 1970 to 1975, gold and silver
coins (minted by governments) appreciated in value
60% annually and real estate appreciated in value 30%
annually, whereas the rate of inflation increased by a
little less than 10%.

Why do paper assets lose value when silver coins,
gold coins and real estate do not? Because sometimes
the government (by printing money) can increase the
supply of paper dollars without limit (reducing the
value of every dollar), whereas it cannot increase the
supply of silver coins, gold coins and real estate without
limit (their supply is limited by the available silver, gold
and land). In other words, the U.S. government causes
inflation. When the government spends more dollars
than it collects in taxes, it makes up for its deficit spending by borrowing money or by printing money. This
increases the number of dollars in circulation and
causes each dollar to buy less goods and services.

When the dollar is backed by either silver or gold (or
any other commodity), the number of dollars that the
government can print is limited by the country's reserves of silver or gold. However, when the dollar is
unbacked, the government can increase the money
supply without limit and inflation can get out of control.

A look at inflationary times in the past will be helpful
in understanding the results of inflation and the circumstances which have led up to the modern age of inflation.

In 1775, during the American Revolution, the Second Continental Congress authorized the first issue of
paper money. Because coins were scarce and being
hoarded, Congress decided to authorize the issue of $2
million of continental bills (paper money) rather than
spend the two million Spanish silver dollar coins held in
the Treasury. But $2 million worth of paper money did
not last long in financing the war, nor did Congress at

that time have the power to raise additional money by taxing. In desperation, Congress authorized the issue of more paper money backed by the full faith of the U.S. continent in anticipation of future taxes. These paper bills could be issued without limit, so, whenever the government needed money, it printed more "continentals." Of course, the more paper money it printed, the less each continental was worth. Even after winning the war, all the measures tried by Congress failed to restore confidence in the inflated continental bills— the damage was already done. People that had placed their savings in continentals were financially ruined, and the popular expression "not worth a continental" was born. In 1787, because of the lack of confidence in unbacked paper currency, the Constitution prohibited states from issuing paper money and made gold and silver coins the only legal tender for the payment of their debts.

But times change and people forget. At the outbreak of the Civil War, Congress again issued unbacked federal notes because the Treasury was almost empty. These paper notes were printed with green ink rather than the usual black ink and so were called "greenbacks." The more greenbacks the government printed, the more it inflated the supply of money and the less each greenback was worth. It got to the point that Californians refused to accept greenbacks as money, and other citizens were demanding $100 worth of greenbacks for $35 worth of gold. Fortunately, the North decided to limit the excessive printing of greenbacks by making them convertible into gold or silver.

The South also issued unbacked paper money—Confederate Treasury Notes. The excessive printing of this unbacked paper money caused inflation in the South to become so rampant that a victim of the times related the following: "Before the Civil War, I went to the market with my money in my pocket and brought back my purchases in a basket, but now, I take my money to the market in a basket and bring home my purchases in my pocket." (Does this sound familiar?)

In 1900, after the Gold Rush, the U.S. government went back on the gold standard, which made dollars convertible into gold. This golden age lasted until 1934, when in the midst of another national crisis, the depression, Congress voted to end the minting of gold coins.

Then, in 1965, Congress voted to reduce the silver in U.S. coins from 90% to 40%, and by 1971, Congress voted to remove all silver from U.S. coins. In addition, you could no longer redeem silver certificates (Federal Reserve Notes) for silver.

In 1971, President Nixon closed the U.S. gold window, ending the convertibility of a dollar into gold. This meant that the U.S. dollar was no longer as good as gold (or silver either!). Once again, the U.S. government could print unbacked paper money without limit. This made it possible for Congress to pay for the unpopular Vietnam War by deficit spending rather than by raising taxes. By 1975, the U.S. government's deficit spending had increased to over $72 billion. Now you know why there are so many dollars in circulation, which, in turn, is why your dollar is losing purchasing power.

On the other hand, the government can only mint silver and gold coins when they have reserves of silver and gold. As a result, coins did not lose their buying power the way paper dollars did. For example, in 1975, a pre-1965 dime consisting of 90% silver was worth more as silver bullion than its 10¢ face value. As a result, these coins were no longer in circulation, and if bought from a coin dealer, a silver dime would cost 30¢ to 35¢ (its approximate value in silver). In other words, two pre-1965 dimes worth 20¢ in 1964 were worth 30¢ to 35¢ in 1975. That is why silver and gold coins offer inflation protection—their buying power remains stable.

Real estate offers similar inflation protection. The government cannot inflate real estate because the amount of real estate is limited by the supply of land. And, of course, it cannot create additional land. Therefore, silver coins, gold coins and real estate are practical ways for the average investor to preserve savings and protect them from the loss of purchasing power during inflationary times.

SILVER AND GOLD COINS

You spend coins constantly, but have you ever taken a close look at U.S. coins? They are beautiful and reveal a good deal about our American heritage. Every coin has the words "United States of America," "Liberty," "In God We Trust" and "E Pluribus Unum" (from many, one). In addition, coins have engravings of symbols of freedom and many of the famous American statesmen. Furthermore, every coin has a mint date and a coin face value—"one cent," "five cents," "one dime," "quarter dollar," "half dollar" and "one dollar."

Actually, what are coins? They are metal minted by the U.S. government for legal tender (money). They are used by people as a medium of exchange as well as a store of value. The United States of America seal on a coin is a guarantee of the purity and weight of the coin's metal content.

The exact metal content of each coin is established by coinage acts passed by Congress. The first Coinage Act was passed in 1792, establishing ten U.S. coins: three gold coins ($10, $5, $2.50 gold pieces); five silver coins (dollar, half dollar, quarter dollar, dime and half dime); and two copper coins (one cent and one-half cent). These coins originally contained metal enough to equal their face value. In 1795, however, Congress ordered the weight of the copper cent reduced because of a copper shortage. The U.S. citizens were incensed and called this "legal robbery." (What would they have said in 1971, when all the silver was removed from U.S. coins?)

In the 1790s, citizens were very aware of the metal content of every coin because goods were bought with silver coins or the metal content of coins (silver and gold bullion). The price of merchandise was quoted by grams or ounces of these metals. Furthermore, citizens could deposit gold or silver bullion with the U.S. Mint and in exchange receive coins of equal weight.

By the early 1800s, the bullion value of gold and silver coins was worth more than their face value. So, coin collectors who studied the science of coins hoarded rare-date coins (years when relatively few coins were minted); speculators hoarded common-date coins for their metal content because they hoped to resell them for a profit as the price of silver and gold increased; and the general public hoarded gold and silver coins because they trusted silver and gold bullion as a store of value. As a result, coins disappeared from circulation and paper money came into use.

In the 1970s, history repeated itself. Silver and gold coins were no longer in circulation for the same reason —their bullion value was worth more than their face value. Furthermore, the government no longer was minting them. If you wanted U.S. silver or gold coins, you had to buy them from coin dealers.

You buy coins for inflation insurance on your paper dollar assets much as you buy fire insurance on your home. You pay a small sum of money every year to insure your home against financial loss in case of fire. Similarly, you set aside a small sum of money (between 5% and 15% of your total assets) in silver and gold coins to insure your paper assets against financial loss in case of rampant inflation. Furthermore, in case you do not need to use your coins during your lifetime, they can be passed on to your heirs for their inflation insurance in the future.

Silver and gold coins offer inflation protection because they contain silver and gold bullion, which does not lose purchasing power with the excess printing of paper dollars. For example, in 1975, when government deficit spending had increased to over $72 billion, paper dollars were so plentiful that 129 to 200 paper dollars were required to buy one ounce of gold, which formerly could be bought with only 35 paper dollars. In 1975, when gold sold for $140 an ounce, the gold content of one $20 U.S. gold piece would buy $140 worth of groceries, or seven times as much as twenty paper dollars would buy. Historically, silver and gold coins have retained their buying power during inflationary times.

Silver Coins for Inflation Insurance

Remember the silver dimes, quarters, half dollars and silver dollars that were minted before 1965? These coins were much heavier than coins minted after 1965 because they were minted from 90% silver. Even the coins minted before 1971 had some silver—40% silver ("clad" coins). But after 1970, U.S. coins contained no silver.

Traditionally, dimes, quarters, half dollars, and dollars minted from silver are good inflation insurance. You can buy them from coin dealers at a price above their silver bullion value (a premium). This premium is determined by the supply and demand for the various silver coins.

U.S. silver dimes, quarters or half dollars are sold in bags. Each bag contains face values of $1,000 (10,000 dimes, 4,000 quarters or 2,000 half dollars). There is no mixing of denominations within a bag. Occasionally, coin dealers sell half bags with face values of $500.

A $1,000 bag of pre-1965 silver coins (minted with

90% silver) contains 715 ounces of silver. Most of these coins are highly circulated (used) and are sold for the small premium of 2% to 4%. For example, if silver sold for $4 an ounce, you would probably pay about $2,920 for a bag of pre-1965 coins whose face value is $1,000 and which contains 715 ounces of silver ($2,860 worth of silver plus a $60 premium).

A $1,000 bag of circulated clad silver coins (minted with 40% silver) contains 290 ounces of silver. Because clad coins were only minted for a few years (1965 to 1970), their supply is more limited, and so they sell for a slightly higher premium (5% to 7%). For example, if silver sold for $4 an ounce, you would probably pay about $1,240 for a bag of clad coins whose face value is $1,000 and which contains 290 ounces of silver ($1,160 worth of silver and an $80 premium).

Although buying bags of U.S. silver dimes, quarters or half dollars is a practical way for the average person to buy inflation insurance, there are inconveniences. They are bulky—each bag of coins requires the storage space of a five-gallon can; and they are heavy—each bag weighs close to sixty pounds.

Coin dealers also sell pre-1936 U.S. silver dollars, which are sold singly, in lots of twenty or in bags of 1,000. A pre-1936 silver dollar (minted with 90% silver) contains a little less than three-quarters of an ounce of silver (.715 ounces). Since the supply of silver dollars is more limited than the supply of pre-1965 silver coins or clad silver coins, they sell for higher premiums (usually premiums of 100% above their silver content). For example, if silver sold for $4 an ounce, you would probably pay about $5 for a pre-1936 used silver dollar which contains about three-quarters of an ounce of silver ($2.86 worth of silver and a $2.14 premium). Low-premium silver dimes, quarters and half dollars offer more inflation protection for their silver content, whereas silver dollars (in excellent condition), because of their scarcity, offer greater potential for appreciating in value as the years go by.

U.S. silver coins, of course, are always worth their face values of 10¢, 25¢, 50¢ or $1. This limits how much U.S. silver coins can decline in value, and yet there is no limit to how much they can increase in value.

Gold Coins for Inflation Insurance

U.S. gold coins, like U.S. silver coins, are no longer in circulation. Gold coins minted by the U.S. government are inflation insurance because U.S. coins are valuable for their gold bullion content. In addition, they are also spendable in the United States. In other words, even if gold bullion loses its value, a $20 gold piece is legal tender of the U.S. government and the U.S. government will redeem them for $20.

The U.S. government stopped minting gold coins in 1933, and as the years go by, U.S. gold coins increase in value because of their scarcity. By 1975, U.S. gold coins were selling for large premiums of 50% or more.

Since it is the gold content (bullion) of a coin that gives you inflation insurance, you will get more gold content for your money by buying lower-premium gold coins. Foreign governments currently mint gold coins which sell for the smaller premiums of 2% to 20%. Three popularly traded foreign gold coins are the South African krugerrand, the Austrian 100 korona and the Mexican 50 pesos.

The European favorite bullion coin (and my favorite too!) is the South African krugerrand, which is unique because it contains exactly one ounce of gold. Its value can be easily determined by checking the market price of one ounce of gold (published daily in newspapers all over the world). The South African government is planning to mint half krugerrands and quarter krugerrands in the future. In 1975, the krugerrand sold for a relatively small premium (4% to 12%). For example, if the

price of gold was $140 an ounce, you would probably
pay about $147.50 for a krugerrand ($140 worth of
gold, because it is exactly one ounce, and the premium
of $7.50).

The Austrian 100 korona contains slightly less than
one ounce of gold (.9802 ounces). In 1975, the korona
was being minted by the Austrian government with a
1915 die (referred to as an official restrike) and was a
good buy because it sold for the smallest premium of
these three foreign gold coins (2% to 8%). For example,
if the price of gold was $140 an ounce you would proba-
bly pay about $141 for an Austrian 100 korona ($137.20
worth of gold and the smaller premium of $2.80).

The Mexican 50 pesos contains over an ounce of gold
(1.2056 ounces) and is a particularly beautiful coin. It is
an official restrike by the Mexican government. In
1975, it sold for the highest premium of these three
foreign gold coins (6% to 20%). For example, if the
price of gold was $140 an ounce, you would probably
pay about $178.50 for a Mexican 50 pesos ($168.70
worth of gold plus the higher premium of $9.80).

How to Buy Silver and Gold Coins

Silver and gold coins are sold by coin dealers. The supply and demand for the various coins determines their
prices. There is a bid price (the price you receive if you
sell coins) and also an asked price (the price you pay if
you buy coins). The difference between the bid and
asked prices is the commission the coin dealer receives,
which usually runs from 2% to 10% depending on the
size of your order. Try not to pay more than 8% commission and don't hesitate to shop around and get two
bids before you buy (or sell) because the coin market is
unregulated. It consists of hundreds of different coin
dealers throughout the United States. It is important to
buy coins only from reputable coin dealers such as U.S.
banks, Swiss banks or individual coin dealers who have

been in business a long time because you want to guard
against buying counterfeit coins.

Silver coins are sold only by individual coin dealers,
whereas gold coins are sold by individual coin dealers
as well as by certain U.S. banks and Swiss banks. Republic National Bank (452 Fifth Avenue, New York, New
York 10018) is the largest gold bullion dealer in the
United States. The bank will sell you a minimum of ten
coins, either U.S. gold coins or popularly traded foreign
bullion coins. The bank will mail these coins to you at
their expense and also will give you a written guarantee
of their authenticity. You can use the bank's toll-free
telephone number (800 223–5578) to place an order.
Furthermore, the bank will repurchase coins at their
current value if you ever want to sell them.

Since you are buying coins for inflation protection,
you want to pay for them in full (coins can be bought
on margin), take physical possession (unless kept by a
Swiss bank) and keep coins in a safe (such as a safety
deposit box) with a record of their cost and their date
of purchase.

**MY CASH Checklist for Buying Gold and Silver
Coins**
Let's briefly review buying gold and silver coins for
inflation protection by using the MY CASH checklist.
Silver and gold coins have no *M*aturity date, pay no
*Y*ield and are not *C*allable. You do not *A*nticipate a
profit or loss because you are buying them strictly as
inflation insurance. The *S*afety of coins depends upon
the future value of silver or gold, but their value can
never decline below the face value of the coin. *H*ow
much liquidity for coins? The bullion coins recommended for inflation protection can usually be sold for
cash immediately.

Shirley Wright Buys Coins for Inflation Insurance
Shirley Wright figures she has about $65,000 worth of
paper assets (a bank account, Treasury notes, Sears Roebuck bonds, PHA municipals, AT&T stock and mutual
funds). Since U.S. government spending is increasing
(causing paper dollars to be more plentiful), she wants
to buy inflation insurance for about $3,250, or 5% of her
paper assets.

In the past, silver and gold coins have provided excellent inflation protection, but, in 1975, there was some
doubt as to whether these coins will continue to be a
store of value because silver and gold are no longer
considered monetary metals (used to back government
currencies). Nevertheless, Shirley believes silver and
gold coins will continue to increase in value as more
paper dollars are circulated. As a matter of fact, this
might be a particularly good time to buy coins because
their doubtful future value has caused their prices to
drop dramatically.

She heads for the coin shop in her neighborhood that
has been in business for as long as Shirley can remember (at least twenty years). She finds out she can buy a
bag of pre-1965 circulated dimes (90% silver) for $2,-
900 or a $1,000 bag of circulated clad half dollars (40%
silver) for $1,200. In addition, she can buy ten kruger-
rands (or more) in excellent condition (uncirculated or
excellent condition make coins more valuable) for $140
each (she likes the krugerrand because it is exactly one
ounce of gold).

After she returns home, she decides to call Republic
National Bank to get another quote on krugerrands.
The bank quotes the same price for uncirculated krugerrands, which they buy directly from the South African government. Since Shirley does not live in New
York State, there will be no sales tax on the coins she
buys from the bank. She orders fifteen krugerrands at

$140 each from the bank, asking for a written guarantee of their authenticity, and then mails a $2,100 check to the bank.

She also buys the bag of clad half dollars from the coin dealer; even if the price of silver declines, the most she can lose is the $200 plus tax she pays above their face value. She arranges to have the coin dealer deliver her coins to the bank, where she gives him a bank check for $1,200 plus sales tax. She places the coins in a medium-size safety deposit box and includes a record of their purchase price and purchase date.

Shirley is satisfied with the purchase of clad half dollars and fifteen krugerrands. This gives her $3,300 worth of inflation insurance on her paper dollar assets —*she is surely right.*

REAL ESTATE

From the cradle to the grave, you use real estate. You are born in real estate (a hospital or home), you live in real estate (a home or apartment building), you work in real estate (a store, office or factory) and you are buried in real estate (the ground). Real estate is a commodity that is limited because the supply of land is limited. As Will Rogers said, "Buy land, they ain't makin' it no more."

The two strongest human desires have been to perpetuate the race and to own land. In olden times, the possession of real estate was taken by force, but gradually law and order prevailed, and the buying and selling of real estate became a respected and well-organized business. In fact, more wealth has been made in real estate than in any other business venture.

Real estate—vacant land, homes or income property (residential, commercial and industrial)—is bought to make a profit, to receive an income, for tax advantages

or as an inflation hedge. We are going to discuss buying
real estate primarily for inflation protection.

During inflationary times, it takes more paper dollars
to buy the commodity of real estate, much as it takes
more paper dollars to buy the commodities of wheat,
sugar, silver or gold. Inflation causes building costs to
increase, which, in turn, causes the value of existing
property to increase. In other words, the value of
money invested in real estate is usually preserved when
inflation causes the value of paper dollars to depreciate.
Furthermore, real estate is usually bought with the
small down payment of about 20%, which allows you to
benefit from the price increase of a large amount of real
estate. In addition, the mortgage (the balance you borrow using the real estate as collateral) is repaid in
monthly payments for up to twenty or thirty years. This
is an inflation hedge because the mortgage will be repaid in the future with cheaper dollars.

But you need an assured income to make mortgage
payments as well as tax payments because these expenses continue in good times and in bad times, that is,
whether the property produces an income or not. Furthermore, the mortgage company and local government have the right to foreclose (take your property) if
these payments are not made, and you stand to lose the
money you have invested in real estate. Therefore, before you buy real estate, ask yourself, "Do I have
enough financial staying power and will I receive good
return (higher than the rate of inflation) from the net
income or net appreciation of this property?" Only if
the answer to both these questions is "yes" can real
estate possibly give you inflation protection.

Vacant Land As Inflation Insurance
Historically, well-selected land has appreciated in value
faster than the rate of inflation. But since land pays no
income, you should not consider buying it unless you

have enough income to pay annual taxes as well as any other expenses until such time as the land can be sold for a profit.

There are millions and millions of acres of vacant land in the United States. Some is agricultural land valued for its productivity and other is urban land valued for the services it can perform, such as residential use, commercial use, industrial use or storage. Since no two parcels of land are alike, there are many suggested ways to select land, such as buying land around airports, close to a new highway or on the outskirts of city suburbs. The best way to select land is to get the finest expert advice you can find (it will be money well spent).

Buying land is not a wise speculation for an inexperienced novice because if you buy undesirable land, you may never be able to sell it. And even when you own desirable land, it sometimes is difficult to find a buyer who will pay you a reasonable price. Good financing, however, usually makes land easier to resell.

Although the profit you receive when you sell land held six months or longer is taxed at one-half the ordinary income tax rate (capital gains rate), and although you are allowed to deduct real estate taxes, interest payments and other expenses on your tax return, tax laws do not allow you to depreciate vacant land (deduct part of its cost every year as a depreciation expense on your tax return).

In spite of all the risks you take when you buy vacant land, if you make a wise purchase, land can be financially rewarding and serve as inflation insurance.

Your Home As Inflation Insurance

Probably the best way for the average person to get inflation protection from real estate is by purchasing a home in a good neighborhood. Traditionally, during inflationary times, homes have appreciated in value much faster than the rate of inflation. For example, from 1955 to 1975, homes increased in value by 190% (a $20,000 house in 1955 would cost $58,000 in 1975).

Owning your own home also has tax benefits—you can deduct interest charges as well as real estate taxes on your tax return. In addition, when your home is mortgaged, you build up equity every month because each mortgage payment reduces the amount of your loan, which is forced savings.

When you buy a home, first you should consider whether or not it fits your needs, and second you should consider its resale value. It is generally easier to resell a home in a desirable area, close to public transportation, close to schools and with reasonable carrying costs (interest charges on the mortgage, taxes, insurance costs, utility costs and maintenance costs). Of course, the general condition in the real estate market at the time you sell has a major influence on the resale value.

A home bought for a relatively reasonable price, financed by a mortgage that does not have an excessive interest rate and that can be maintained comparatively inexpensively will usually offer you enjoyment and inflation protection.

Income Property As Inflation Insurance
Income property (such as apartment buildings, office buildings and even houses that are rented) must be financially sound in order to give inflation protection. Financially sound income property should produce a fair return on your cash down payment, at least 1% more than Treasury bonds currently yield. After all, when you own income property you are required to do additional work which should be rewarded with additional income.

In the 1970s, the price of income property was so inflated that it could no longer produce reasonable yields. People were buying income property as a tax shelter because this type of real estate can be depreciated. Lawyers, doctors and businesspeople making large incomes paid excessive prices for real estate for the sole purpose of deducting large depreciation expenses from their income, which, in turn, would put them in a lower tax bracket. This increased the demand for income real estate and forced prices unrealistically high.

But, in 1975, Congress was considering a bill which would allow the depreciation expense from a building to be used only as a tax deduction from the rental income that building produces. If this bill is passed, income property would lose some of its "tax appeal" and probably sell at more reasonable prices.

A practical way for the average investor to receive income as well as inflation protection is to buy a small apartment building and live in one apartment. This apartment building can contain three, six or even ten units (whatever you can afford). You must be prepared to keep books, collect rents and put up with the nuisance of managing property. Select the neighborhood you want to live in and make sure the vacancy rate is low. Then, carefully estimate the income you will receive after deducting expenses (taxes, interest, insurance, utilities, maintenance, repairs and depreciation). Be sure to deduct another 5% to 10% for a vacancy allowance (even if the building is completely rented when you buy it) and set aside another 5% to 10% for a major repair fund. You need an adequate net return from residential income property as well as good management because expenses have been rising faster than rents.

On the other hand, commercial or industrial property with net leases with tenants taking top credit ratings (AAA) requires little or no management. This means the tenant pays all the expenses and whatever rent you receive is your income to keep. But unless the lease calls for the rent to increase with the cost of living, you have no inflation protection. In other words, a building leased for a long time at a fixed rate of rent is similar to buying a long-term bond that pays a fixed rate of interest. Furthermore, commercial and industrial buildings with long-term leases are often single-purpose buildings, which makes them difficult to rent in the future to another tenant. If you buy such a building, when the lease expires you may be required to come up with a large amount of money to make necessary alterations to the interior of the building in order to make it useful for another tenant.

You should also be aware that net leases and the credit ratings of tenants are sometimes misrepresented. After you buy the building (unless you have a lawyer read the fine print), you may find out you have a net lease that requires you to maintain the parking lot, repair the roof or make major repairs, which would reduce your income by a large percentage. In addition, although the credit ratings of tenants are represented as AAA, Standard & Poor, Moody's or Dun & Bradstreet would not rate them that high.

Well-selected income property which produces an income that is higher than the rate of inflation will give you inflation protection as well as tax savings (from depreciation) and forced savings (by reducing your mortgage with monthly payments).

How to Buy Real Estate
The real estate market is a jungle that takes advantage of your lack of knowledge. Therefore, before you buy real estate, locate a reputable real estate agent, one who has been in business a long time and who knows property values in the area that interest you. In addition, whenever possible, have an expert from the American Institute of Real Estate Appraisals (check the yellow pages of the phone book) appraise property for

you and give you an idea of its resale value. It is also a
good idea to pay a builder to check the construction
and condition of any building you are considering. Furthermore, it might be helpful to consult a real estate
lawyer or accountant who has no financial interest in
whether or not you buy the property.

You can't just go out and buy real estate with the idea
that if things don't work out, you'll sell, because there
isn't a ready market for real estate like there is for
securities. It may take months or years before you can
sell real estate at what you consider is a reasonable
price. In addition, buying real estate costs more than
buying securities because commissions are higher (usually 10% or more) and escrow fees and other fees (lawyer, builder or accountant fees) are sometimes necessary expenses.

MY CASH Checklist for Real Estate

Let's briefly review real estate by using the MY CASH
checklist. Real estate has no *M*aturity date. Only income property pays a *Y*ield. Real estate is not *C*allable.
You *A*nticipate a profit if the value of your real estate
increases in the future and a loss if the value of your
property decreases in the future. The *S*afety of real
estate depends on the location of the property and on
the real estate market in general. Furthermore, the
safety of income property is affected by how efficiently
it is managed. *H*ow much liquidity for real estate? You
may be lucky and find a buyer immediately when you
want to sell real estate, but generally it takes a long
time to find a potential buyer willing to pay what you
believe is a reasonable price.

Shirley Wright Buys a Small Apartment Building

Shirley Wright had just received another rent increase,
her third in three years. She decides to inquire about
buying a two-, three- or four-unit apartment building in

her neighborhood. Her present neighborhood is convenient and the vacancy rate is relatively low. Rather than deteriorating, this area is improving because many of the older run-down buildings are being torn down and replaced with expensive new ones.

After talking to friends, neighbors, her lawyer and accountant, Shirley locates two reputable real estate agents that specialize in apartment buildings in her neighborhood. She alerts them as to what she is looking for. She wants a good investment, and since she is going to live on the premises, she also wants a comfortable home. Shirley realizes this will take time to find, especially at the right price.

The two agents show her many buildings. Although they are not what Shirley wants each time, she learns something new about apartment buildings. This is an education in itself.

About eight months later, an agent shows her a three-unit building. Although the apartment building is not exactly what she wants, it will suit her needs. The owner's suite (which she will move into) is tastefully decorated but much smaller than she originally hoped for, and the kitchen needs modernizing. The building is well built (brick with a slate roof and copper plumbing), will require a minimum of maintenance and appears in excellent repair. Nevertheless, she has a reputable builder and appraiser check it thoroughly. She also likes the fact that each tenant pays his or her own utilities.

The owner will finance the building at a relatively reasonable mortgage rate. Furthermore, she only needs a $15,000 down payment and the balance is paid in monthly payments over twenty-five years. Shirley plans to raise this $15,000 by selling her Sears bonds and $5,000 worth of Treasury notes.

Shirley decides to consult with her accountant before making an offer. The rents appear reasonable for that neighborhood, and after deducting the expenses submitted by the real estate agent from the rental income, the accountant also deducts another 5% for a vacancy allowance, 5% for a major repair fund and depreciation expense (which was not listed). Taking into consideration the cost of remodeling the kitchen in her own suite, she makes an offer on the apartment building which will give her a fair return on her down payment.

Shirley buys the building but pays a little more than her original offer. She knows owning an apartment building will require work but the $15,000 she is investing will not depreciate in value if additional paper dollars are printed. Furthermore, in twenty-five years (about the time she hopes to retire), she will own a $100,000 apartment building free and clear and will receive a monthly income from the other two apartments in the building. This is worth working for—*she is surely right.*

10

Getting It
All Together

You're now well prepared to go investment shopping.
You have the information and tools you need to compare investments so that you can determine the best
value for the amount of money you have to invest. You
can use the MY CASH checklist (see page 46) to compare all investments, those we have discussed as well as
any we have not talked about. In general, it is more
profitable to loan your money (buy bank time deposits,
government securities, agency securities, municipal
securities, corporate bonds) when the economy is slow-
ing and interest rates are high, and it is more profitable
to own with your money (buy stocks, real estate, warrants, call options, commodity futures) when the economy is expanding and interest rates are low.

If you are loaning your money, and reinvesting the
interest you're paid, the magic number 72 will tell you
immediately how long it will take for your money to
double. For example, if you're paid 9% interest, you
divide 9 into 72 and the answer is 8, which means your
money will double in approximately eight years.

Although *Dollars and ene* uses 1975 figures as ex-
amples, you can substitute the figures for any year you
have money to invest because the basic principles re-
main the same. Now that you have a framework of
reference for investing, you will find the news items on

262

the financial page of your city newspaper more meaningful. Try to keep current with economic trends by setting aside an hour a week to read the *Wall Street Journal, Barron's Financial Weekly, Forbes* magazine, *Fortune* magazine, *Money* magazine, the business section of *Time* magazine or *Newsweek* magazine, investment letters and even by listening to the weekly television show "Wall Street Week" on the Public Broadcasting System.

Record keeping for your investments is very important. You may already have a system that works for you, but if you need a simplified way to keep investment records, copy the way Shirley Wright keeps her records. Shirley divides her record keeping into three categories: Assets, Income and Profit & Loss. Incidentally, she keeps these records in pencil, so when she sells an investment she can merely erase it under "Assets" and list it under "Profit & Loss."

In case Shirley should lose her bankbook or any of her certificates (for securities), she likes to have a record of their receipt numbers, which are listed in a column under "Assets". Furthermore, since income (interest and dividend) is paid either every three months or every six months, Shirley finds it easier to keep her income record in six-month pairs. In other words, she keeps the income for January and July in one column. That way, she only needs six columns for income rather than twelve (one for each month).

It might puzzle you when you see Shirley lists $5,000 worth of Treasury notes under "Assets" (bought 5/1/75) as well as $5,000 worth of Treasury notes under "Profit & Loss" (bought the same day but sold 11/20/75). The reason for this is that Shirley originally bought $10,000 worth of these Treasury notes. Subsequently, when she bought an apartment building, she sold $5,000 worth. Since she still owns $5,000 worth of Treasury notes, they are listed under "Assets"; and

ASSETS

	Purchase Date	Purchase Price	Maturity Date	Redemption Price	Receipt Number
Sound Nat'l. Bank	2-1-74	$1,500		$1,500	21075
Savings Bonds—H	9-1-74	$1,000	2-1-83	$1,000	265432H
Swiss Bank Corp.	9-1-74	14,000 Sfr.		14,000 Sfr.	57.127
Treasury Notes	9-1-75	$11,000	9-1-77	$11,000	912827
Treasury Notes	5-1-75	$5,000	5-1-80	$5,000	912793
Agency Securities	1-7-75	$5,025	1-1-78	$5,000	Held at bank
PHA Bonds	4-1-75	$10,000	4-1-95 (1990-call)	$10,000	71 through 75
Apt. Bldg.	12-1-75	$15,000 dwn.			
AT&T Stock	7-10-75	$4,272			
Clad Coins (bag)	11-22-75	$2,900			
15 Krugerrands	12-5-75	$2,100			

INCOME

	January & July	February & August	March & September	April & October	May & November	June & December
Sound Nat'l. Bank 5½%	$41.25					
	$41.25					
Savings Bonds 6%		$21*				
		$21*				
Swiss Bank Corp. 5½%			$440*			272 Sfr.
Treasury Notes 8%			$440*			

	Purchase Date	Sale Date	Purchase Price	Sale Price	Gain	Loss
Treasury Notes 8%					$200*	$200*
Agency Securities 8½%	$212.50*	$212.50*				
PHA Bonds 6½%				$325‡	$325‡	
Apt. Bldg.		$100	$100	$100	$100	$100
AT&T Stock	$85†			$85		
Option Income		$175				

PROFIT & LOSS

	Purchase Date	Sale Date	Purchase Price	Sale Price	Gain	Loss
3,000 Swiss Francs	9-1-74	4-20-75	$1,050	$1,205	$185§	
Treasury Notes	8-1-74	5-25-75	$10,000	$10,270	$270§	
Investment Co. Stock	6-23-74	6-27-75	$4,893	$5,885	$1,062§	
AT&T Warrants	1-6-75	10-8-75	$390	$2,925	$2,535§	
Sears Bonds	5-1-75	11-29-75	$10,000	$9,975		$25
Treasury Notes	5-1-75	11-20-75	$5,025	$4,995		$35

*Exempt from state and local income taxes.

†The first $100 in stock dividends is exempt from federal income tax.

‡Exempt from state, local and federal income taxes.

§Long-term capital gain or loss (held over six months).

since she sold $5,000 worth of Treasury notes, they are
listed under "Profit & Loss." In all other ways, Shirley
Wright's record keeping is self-explanatory.

As you build an investment program throughout
your life, the following Ten Investment Command-
ments will help you keep on the straight and narrow
path of sound investing.

I The basis of every investment decision should
be to try to preserve your money.

II The word *guarantee* is only as valuable as the
financial condition and trustworthiness of the individual, government or corporation giving the guarantee.

III Buy investments that do not cause you undue
anxiety.

IV Judge investment on facts—not on tips, rumor
or emotion.

V Do not buy an investment you do not
thoroughly understand.

VI Use the MY CASH checklist (see page 46) to
compare investments so that you can determine
the better buy.

VII Deal only with reputable and financially
sound people and corporations (banks, brokerage
firms, real estate firms, coin dealers, etc.).

VIII Investing requires patience—don't try to
achieve too much too fast.

IX Do not discuss your investments with friends.
Investing is a personal decision and what is good
for them is not necessarily good for you.

X Don't neglect your investments. Since the
value of investments changes constantly, they
need periodic checkups. Take good care of your
investments, and they will take good care of you.

ABOUT THE AUTHOR

BETTY WULIGER was graduated from the University of Illinois with honors and was elected to Phi Beta Kappa. She has had practical experience in both sides of the investment business—investing as an individual in real estate and securities and selling as a professional stockbroker—as well as working as a business consultant. She was also a member of the Cleveland Society for Financial Analysts. On retiring in 1971, she and her husband moved to Southern California.